Turpin. P.

Lambert J.ᵉ sculp.

CACAO.

a. l. l.

CHOCOLATE
RUNS THROUGH MY VEINS

The Insightful History of the Women of Chocolate

By

CONNIE SPENUZZA, M.S.Ed.

Project Photographer: Lisa Renee Baker

Library of Congress Control Number: 2021953180

ISBN: 978-0-9987031-6-9

Printed in the United States of America

For my pride and joy:
Lana, Roman, Siena

Contents

Tragic Aroma

*I*T WASN'T THE EVER-SO-SLIGHT SERPENTINE MOTION OF THE EMERALD TREE BOA that startled Federico. Nor was it the parade of giant tarantula spiders that marched ominously along the mushy mulch of the cacao tree leaves that made him bolt. It was the swift gleam of the machete, already dripping with a blood-red substance, that did him in. By the time I reacted, and wiped the sweat that trickled from my forehead into my irritated eyes, all I could see was Federico's bristly brown fur as he tumbled violently over the boulders strewn along the currents of the Babahoyo River in my native Ecuador's lowland rainforest.

FIG. 1

Minutes before our pet capuchin monkey's demise, nearly seventy years ago, my cousins and I cautiously crossed the fragile and ancient rope-suspension bridge over the river. We stomped uphill, eager to chomp on the sweet white pulp of freshly cut cacao pods. Despite our sadness over Federico, we couldn't wait to rudely spit the cacao's bitter seeds at each other, in the inconsiderate manner of entitled young brats. The workers on our family's hacienda took Federico's drowning as yet another tragic act of nature, but they were kind enough to hand us coconut water and fresh papaya slices to sweeten the stream of our salty tears. Between my childish sobs, I realized that I had always understood Federico's clever mind. He had undoubtedly smelled monkey blood on the machete, the same machete now used to cut the cacao pods for us to taste. He didn't want to be the blade's next victim.

FIG. 2

My gloomy mood was not only caused by the loss of our rambunctious pet. Just the previous day, I'd spent six confusing hours with my great-aunt. I accompanied her to the hut of a renowned natural healer from the indigenous Tsáchila ethnic group. The Tsáchila of Santo Domingo de los Colorados were known throughout South America for their decorative face paint, originally applied to ward off European smallpox; and for their application of achiote, the ground annatto seed paste that transformed their black hair into a stiff, bright red helmet.

While I waited outside, I was offered a chunk of rough and tasteless chocolate candy that was locally made. Although just a child, I had already developed a

FIG. 3

discriminating palete for the exquisite Belgian chocolate that my elegant grandfather served me, along with thin shavings of Manchego cheese, in our family's estate in the capital city of Quito, high up in the Andes Mountains. I set the country-bumpkin chocolate on the ground, and peeked into the hut. The fierce appearance of the shaman didn't alarm me: I'd seen him at work on one or another of my aunts many times before. What unnerved me was my great-aunt's uncontrolled wailing, and the pungent scent of chocolate emanating from her body. I never discovered what the healer told her or what treatment he performed on her, but she lived to the ripe age of ninety-eight.

It's been many decades since Federico's untimely death left a visceral tattoo on my heart. Ever since that sultry morning, no matter where I am in the world, with each bite of bitter dark chocolate I chew, I'm transported back to that specific dense canopy of the cacao trees, not far from the hot and steamy tribal lands of the Tsáchila people. The acrid odors of decaying fruit, wet leaves, and remnants of a partially consumed Giant Armadillo are burnished in my sense of smell. However, I cherish the memory of the fluttering wings of the immense iridescent blue butterflies, now sadly endangered, as they flitted past red and bumpy cacao pods—the size of papayas—on their way towards the sinister river.

Years later, I realized that I had witnessed a marvel of nature that day: I saw hundreds of gigantic, blue butterflies that my grandchildren will never see, zooming past the finest aromatic Arriba Nacional cacao in the world. For me, this is simultaneously a dreadful and a heartwarming memory, since my mind conflates cacao with both joy and tragedy, with the uncontrollable forces of nature, and with the primordial connection of cacao to the indigenous people of Ecuador and the Americas. Those two days primed me to recognize the fullness of cacao and thus of chocolate, in its universal significance to people throughout the world. Under the sweltry canopy of the most fragrant *pepas de oro*, the golden seeds of cacao, I tasted the pleasure—and understood the tragic and fortunate paradox that has always been chocolate.

FIG. 4

FIG. 5

Ambrosial Magnetism

Throughout the millennia, cacao's ambrosial magnetism has drawn people to cultivate and process it, and to drink it during solemn rituals. Its scientific name, *Theobroma cacao*, comes from ancient Greek and translates as "Food for the Gods." In its first documented history, it was ceremoniously consumed in chocolate drink form by the elite of Mesoamerica. Today, eaten in its many chocolate forms, it is the most popular sweet treat in the world.

FIG. 6

Countless books abound on the subject of chocolate—from cookbooks to scholarly tomes to mystery novels. What makes this book unique is my first-hand experience with chocolate over seventy years; and, specifically, my knowledge of the international history of the women of chocolate. I was born in Ecuador, the original land of chocolate, and spent many school vacations on my family's cacao and banana haciendas. My knowledge of Spanish culture, combined with my years of living with Spanish nuns in Quito's Sisters of Mercy convent school, informed my understanding of how chocolate could be kept a secret in the sixteenth century by the powerful monasteries and convents of Spain.

As a university student in France in the early 1970s, I journeyed throughout Europe on a scholarly genealogical hunt for my roots. I was searching for knowledge about my Basque ancestor Ojer de Velástegui, a teenage scribe from a noble family of Guipúzcoa, who journeyed aboard the *Pinta* on Christopher Columbus' famed 1492 expedition to the Americas. It wasn't until 1992, five-hundred years after the *Pinta* arrived in America, that I finally found my direct connection to Ojer de Velástegui—when I was tempted by the scent of melted chocolate wafting from a tiny confectionary in Tolosa, a small town in the Basque country of Spain.

Through my Basque ancestor, I learned about the long history of chocolate and the Basques of Spain and France. Painfully, I also learned about the

Alhambra Decree of 1492 that expelled 200,000 Jewish people from Spain.[1] This cataclysmic event had repercussions for the subsequent trade of chocolate by the Ladino-speaking Sephardic Jewish merchants of Curaçao and the Caribbean, Rhode Island, and New York. Further fanaticism by the Spanish Crown and the Tribunal of the Holy Office of the Inquisition led to the burning at the stake of Basque women accused of witchcraft; the torture and murder of Jewish people for practicing their faith; and the severe punishment of women in Mexico who were accused of sorcery because of their knowledge of chocolate, herbal medicine, and poisonous substances.

For sixty years, I have been privileged to travel to more than 127 countries throughout the world. For several years we owned a house in Mexico, but it's been my numerous study visits to the many archaeological sites and historic centers of Mexico and Guatemala that taught me about the promulgation of chocolate, and its primary importance to the ancient people of Mesoamerica.

From their pictograph codices that managed to survive the fanatical burning by the Spanish, to the carved stone of the many remarkable archaeological sites in Central America,

FIG. 7

FIG. 8

to the chronicles written by sixteenth-century Spanish explorers and clergy, along with my lifelong independent study, I have found remarkable women linked to the history of chocolate of Central America.

The religious women cooped up in convents in Spain and Mexico throughout the ages led the way in the creation and development of chocolate confections. As far back as the eleventh century, the nuns of the Convent of San Clemente in Toledo, Spain are generally given the credit for creating marzipan, the delicious treat of honey and almond fame. This no doubt reflects the Arab cultural influence in Spain during and after their 781-year reign: the Arab use of almonds and honey in desserts must have led to the good nuns of San Clemente to create their famous confection. The ingenious confections and desserts devised by nuns—like *suspiros de monja* (nun's sighs) and *huesos de santo* (bones of a saint)—have been famous in the Hispanic world for centuries. The credit for creating chocolate confections should be given to the religious women who supported their convents through their sweet inventions.

This book links the nuns who created chocolate confectionary to women accused of sorcery because of their knowledge of chocolate and natural healing; to the noble women of the royal courts of Europe who spearheaded the chocolate-drinking craze of the seventeenth century; to the women who were branded and imprisoned for their chocolate larceny—and, to those women throughout history, who in fact, did employ chocolate and poison as an instrument of revenge.

While I rejoice in the success of the women entrepreneurs of the nineteenth century who established chocolate empires, and brought their originality

FIG. 9

to chocolate production, I remain dejected at the plight of modern-day child workers in the chocolate industry. In *The Hidden Ingredient in Chocolate: Africa's Child Slaves*, Sabrina Pecorelli writes:

> Smugglers are paid to traffic children from countries like Mali and Guinea into the Ivory Coast, Ghana, and Algeria. After they are handed off to farmers, the children are forced to work long hours in life-threatening conditions, carrying heavy bags of cocoa seeds, using sharp machetes, and climbing tall trees without equipment. They are beaten with bicycle chains or cacao branches if they fail to meet required quotas or attempt an escape. These children are physically and psychologically abused and deprived of their childhoods to lay the foundation for other countries' luxurious consumption of chocolate.[2]

FIG. 10

Chocolate's Origin in Ecuador

$\mathcal{F}$OR CENTURIES, CHRONICLERS, HISTORIANS, ARCHAEOLOGISTS, AND SCIENTISTS asserted that cacao originated in Mesoamerica. In 2018, news of a scientifically proven new origin for the world's most coveted sweet erupted like a giant molten-chocolate volcano. The announcement revealed that an international team of scientists and scholars found traces of cacao dating back 5,300 years at the Santa Ana-La Florida archeological site in southeastern Ecuador, located 3,412 feet above sea level. This is where prime Nacional cacao is grown.

FIG. 11

The team uncovered cacao tinged, stone and ceramic vessels 1,700 years older than evidence of cultivation of cacao in Mesoamerica. Geneticist Claire Lanaud said they found evidence of cocoa use "by analysing the starch grains characteristic of the genus Theobroma, traces of theobromine, a biochemical compound specific to mature cocoa beans, and ancient cocoa DNA found in ceramic vessels, some of which dated back more than 5300 years." Those vessels came from either tombs or domestic settings, so clearly "cocoa was used both as a funerary offering and for daily consumption."[3]

The site also revealed seashells from the Pacific coast, suggesting trade and communication links between the peoples of the Pacific coast and those of the Amazon. The Mayo Chinchipe people of the western Amazon highlands may have been instrumental, the study contended, in domesticating cocoa in general and the Nacional variety in particular.[4]

Dunn, a science writer and professor of geography, argues that "two factors generally create the conditions necessary for millennia-long preservation of accurate oral histories: specialized story-keepers and cultural isolation."[5]

Note: The terms "cocoa bean" and "cacao bean" are interchangeable.

Cacao beans typically grow within 20 degrees of the equator. This region is commonly referred to as the "cacao belt," and the entire country of Ecuador falls within this cacao growing region. While scientists continue with the arduous excavation and analysis of the Santa Ana–La Florida site, the accepted approach is to wait for their further findings. It seems likely that the scientists will find results that confirm ancestral knowledge. In fact, intangible forms of heritage such as oral transmission of knowledge and the presence of human descendants in the areas in question could be as invaluable to advance knowledge as scientific research there.

❈ ❈ ❈

As a child in Quito in the early 1950s, my indigenous nanny often told me that her ancestors were the Chachapoya people—the "Warriors of the Clouds"— who lived more than 1000 years ago far south near the Utcubamba River. She often hummed a melancholy tune and told me that her ancestors were buried high in the cliffs. She vowed that one day she would go there to pay her respects. Many decades later, in 2006, scientists found 1000-year-old mummies of the Chachapoya Cloud People in a mountain ridge near the Utcubamba River. The sarcophagi, their red-hued designs still vis-

FIG. 12

FIG. 13

ible, contained humanoid faces. Chachapoya buildings were uncovered that were over 1000 years old and contained rock paintings.

My unschooled nanny tolerated years of ridicule from the rest of the domestic staff for her seemingly outlandish claims, and did not live long enough to be vindicated. By the time scientific proof of her Chachapoya ancestors was announced, I had lived in California for forty years, but I rejoiced at the news. It was testimony to my former nanny's tenacity and authenticity, and I vowed to respect such remarkable kernels of truth from people some "experts" might regard as insignificant and unreliable sources.

FIG. 14

When we compare elements of the culture of the ancient indigenous people of the Ecuadorian Amazon rainforest basin with the cultural history of the more recent past, by studying the inhabitants of the same geographical area, we can form more educated premises. The ethnic group that has inhabited the Amazon River basin for thousands of years was given the pejorative name of *jívaro* by the Spanish, primarily because they were fierce warriors who refused to be dominated. Their knowledge of the rivers and tributaries, dense rainforests, immense waterfalls, and the rugged Andean landscapes enabled them to evade the Spanish. This semi-nomadic group has been divided into four sub-groups by geographic territory, ranging from the Amazon River basin of southeastern Ecuador to the foothills of the Andes. Each sub-group inhabited regions rich in fresh water, fauna and flora to guarantee their survival.

The modern-day nomenclature given to the culture of the Amazon basin of southeastern Ecuador that first cultivated cacao is the Mayo Chinchipe-Marañon. In the past it was argued that the soil in the region could not sustain agricultural production, but current evidence gathered from the Santa-Ana-La Florida (3500 BCE) archaeological site reveals something different. Archaeologist Francisco Valdez believes that "Amazonians found ways to overcome the flaws and develop adequate strategies for sustainable food production. Recent studies show that early complexity was present in the tropics with forms of typical Formative period technologies and practices, such as pottery, polished stone artifacts or long distance exchange networks."[6]

The United Nation Educational, Scientific and Cultural Organization agrees that the Ecuadorian southeastern region of the Amazon basin was the home of the Mayo Chinchipe-Marañon culture. It states that this culture lasted approximately 4000 years, and that there is evidence that the ancestors of the Shuar people occupied this region.[7]

My connection to the Shuar people of the Amazon basin began in the 1950s—with my white-knuckle fear of them. They were notorious for their practice of shrinking the heads of their slain adversaries in a laborious and mystical process. The Shuar believed that shrinking an enemy's head meant they could capture his evil spirit and prevent it from seeking revenge.

FIG. 15

FIG. 16

This practice, known as *tsantsa*, felt perilously close to my family. We had an uncle who was the blonde accountant for a Dutch oil company drilling in Shuar territory. For months we did not hear from our uncle who was living incommunicado in the Pasto River, but we joked that he had better be wearing a hat at all times to cover his blonde hair. He could have easily been perceived as an adversary to the Shuar since the oil drilling, drop by drop, damaged their environment and their culture.

My uncle returned to Quito safely, and he even brought back souvenir shrunken heads—squirrel monkeys, not people. But the proximity to these *tsantsas* resulted in immense fear among our indigenous staff and all of us young children, since our older cousins hid the *tsantsas* under our pillows to tease us. The practice of human head shrinking wasn't outlawed until the 1960s. Only now are museums and universities in the United States finally repatriating the human remains, the *tsantsas*, from their collections.[8]

The Shuar did not have a written language, but passed their knowledge orally. Spanish chroniclers as far back as the 1550s describe the Shuar as an untamable people for their refusal to cooperate with the Spanish. In 1559 the Shuar massacred all the Spaniards on their lands for forcing them to work the gold mines. After the massacre, the Shuar dispersed to more inaccessible, hidden rainforests, regaining a sovereignty they maintained until the nineteenth century.[9] Today they lead the indigenous ethnic groups of Ecuador in activism, determined to protect their territory and argue for their independent rule. In 2019, the Shuar brought attention to the global ecological consequences of the large-scale gold

FIG. 17

and copper mining currently undertaken by foreign interests along with the government of Ecuador in what is left of the pristine Shuar rainforests. The Shuar believe that such mining will devastate the Amazon basin and have serious consequences for the world's environment.

After the momentous 2018 scientific finding of the Ecuadorean origins of cacao near the ancient territory of the proto-Shuar people, I experienced my own aha moment. I realized that ever since my early childhood days, when I devoured the sweet cacao pulp from the ripe pods in my family's hacienda, I've been curiously, continuously, and coincidentally intertwined with chocolate for decades. I've read countless books and academic journals on cacao and chocolate, and traveled to the fabled chocolate centers worldwide, and found my ninety-six-year-old step-dad to be a fountain of knowledge due to his remarkable intelligence and memory. As a young boy, back in the 1920s, he panned for gold, along with his revolver-toting adventurer father, in the southern regions of Ecuador, near the territory of the Shuar people. Later, as an engineering student, he moved first to Quito, then to Chile and finally the United States. His vivid descriptions of the topography, the vegetation, and the way the local women processed cacao into chocolate from the cacao trees grown in their small plots of land, was a unique, first-hand account of the laborious ways of the pre-industrial past in Ecuador.

Furthermore, the oral traditions about the value of cacao that were passed down to him by his grandmother, and to her, by her great-grandmother, made the world of chocolate very personal and immediate—despite the fact that I was hearing narratives about an insulated way of life nearly three-hundred-years old. The rhythm of everyday life had not changed much between my dad's life as a young boy in the still-intact rainforests of southern Ecuador and that of his great-grandmother's recounting of her ancestor's life of natural abundance generations before her. It was not difficult for me to form a specific opinion about the history of chocolate based on familial experiences, on my dedicated study, and on my knowledge of life on a desolate cacao hacienda. I surmised that the Shuar of the nineteenth century were likely to be of a very similar culture to their proto-Shuar ancestors who had also gone deeper into the more inaccessible rainforests to avoid their enemies.

In 1989, I received a telephone call from a young Shuar leader visiting the Los Angeles area on a fundraising trip. We had several long conversations about the impending catastrophe of the Amazon River basin, and I connected him to a Southern California church group eager to help. I continued with my typical American life, oblivious about the young Shuar on a mission to seek help for his people, until I read an article about the research of Dr. Sonia Zarrillo and her team. In fragments of ancient DNA, traces of cacao-tree starch grains and theobromine residue, they found enough evidence to say *Theobroma cacao* "was used in Ecuador by 5,450–5300 cal. Yr BP, predating its earliest known use in Central America and Mexico by approximately 1.5 millenia."[10]

✳ ✳ ✳

FIG. 18

FIG. 19

As some of the artifacts from Santa Ana-La Florida have links to the Pacific coast, the researchers suggest that the tree either "spread or was traded into Meso-america."[11] UNESCO also supports the belief that the Mayo Chinchipe-Marañon culture "took plants such as manioc and cocoa to the Coast," and that "cocoa was domesticated in the upper Amazon region, and was taken from there to Central America."[12]

The stone and ceramic vessels found in the Santa Ana-La Florida archeo-logical site, with cacao residue, appear to be from 3200 BCE. During this same era, the Valdivia culture of coastal Ecuador was thriving—creating tools planting crops and engaging in commerce. Its famed Venus figurines remain the earliest representational images found in the Americas.

The idea of cacao's voyage north from Ecuador to Central America in-trigued me. Both scholars and UNESCO supported the concept of trade be-tween these two ancient cultures. Yet, a survey of the academic journals on this subject was very limited. I couldn't imagine finding the data that would connect the trade of cacao over such a vast period of time, especially since the first men-tion of Ecuadorian coastal traders who sailed on balsa wood rafts did not appear until the sixteenth century.

For academics to further advance the scholarship on the Mayo Chinchipe-Marañon culture will be a long an arduous process. It may take many years for research and findings to explain cacao's probable voyage from the Amazon basin to Mesoamerica. Based on my understanding of the Shuar culture, and on my belief that ancestral oral knowledge is indeed a treasure trove, I'm emboldened

FIG. 20

to propose a possibility of the exchange that may have occurred, over millennia, between the proto-Shuar and the cultures of Mesoamerica.

Consider the solid probability that the ancient Shuar women were the ones who cultivated the cacao. To this day, the Shuar comply with their ancient traditions, such as a specific division of labor.[13] Women continue to tend the crops, particularly the manioc and cacao. Up until the recent past, the Shuar women were also known as fierce combatants.

Their knowledge and use of the frog poison they applied in their blow darts is widely recognized as extremely lethal. However, it is unlikely that the proto-Shuar women were involved in the transportation of trade goods since the male Shuar continue to be the principal navigators.

The stone and ceramic vessels found in the Santa Ana-La Florida contain traces of cacao, used both for daily consumption and ceremonial purposes. The daily life of the adult males was to hunt in dense rainforest land or in boats along the many rivers: a daily chocolate drink must have given them stamina.[14] Equally, the women would have

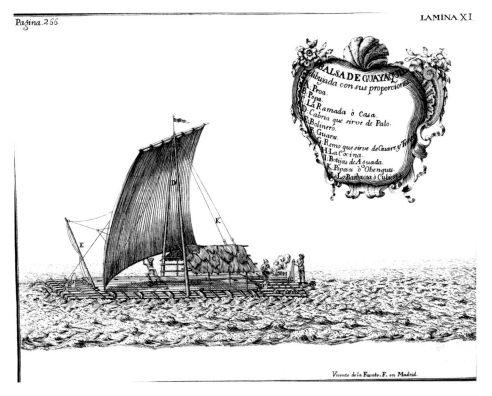

FIG. 21

needed to consume it, to sustain the arduous process of transforming the cacao beans into chocolate, along with their additional duties of food providing, child rearing, and medicinal responsibilities. Centuries later, my dad only saw women working the small cacao groves along the same region of the ancient Shuar.

The late Donald Lathrap, an archaeologist and professor of anthropology, suggested that the coastal Valdivia-Machalilla culture continuum (4000-1500BCE) "represents a westward expansion of a developed form of Tropical Forest Culture."[15] This particular Tropical Forest Culture, originating from the Amazon River basin, was the "mother culture." Lathrap posited that long-distance trade networks from Ecuador to Mexico were most likely coastwise navigation rather than overland travel.[16] Other scholars support this theory, citing evidence that Ecuadorian traders established maritime commercial routes extending from Chile to Colombia, and farther north to Mexico."[17]

It is probable that the balsa log rafts that plied the Pacific Coast in 100 BCE were very similar to those used by the traders of the more ancient Ecuadorian coastal cultures. In 1534, Spanish chronicler Miguel de Este wrote about the balsa log rafts he saw along the Ecuadorian coast:

> These balsas are of some very thick and long wooden logs, which are as soft and light on water as cork. They lash them very tightly with a kind of hemp rope, and above them they place a high framework so that the merchandise and things they carry do not get wet. They set a mast in the largest log in the middle, hoist a sail and navigate all along this

FIG. 22

coast. They are very safe vessels because they cannot sink or capsize, since the water washes through them everywhere.[18]

Based on the documented trading timelines, maritime traders from 100 BCE would have been from the Jama-Coaque culture (100BCE-500CE). This ethnic group lived along the northern coast in the Esmeraldas Province to the central coast of Manabí near Bahía de Caraquez, and were renowned for their exquisite gold earrings, necklaces, and for their detailed ceramic figurines and vessels.

It is interesting to compare the many similarities between the early formative stirrup-spout bottles from Ecuador. Up until 2018, the oldest stirrup spout vessel in the New World was from the coastal Ecuadorian Machalilla culture (1800 to 1500 BCE). But at the Santa Ana-La Florida site, early human effigy, stirrup spout bottles are 5,300 years old, and contain ancient chocolate DNA. Therefore, it appears that the latter served as prototypes for the formerly oldest stirrup-spout bottle in the New World.

Although it is interesting to speculate on the trajectory of cacao from its origins in Ecuador, based on oral tradition and knowledge, on emerging scholarship, and on the information provided by the indigenous culture that has remained in situ for centuries, it is prudent to wait for scholars and scientists to find further evidence of the maritime trade of cacao from its origin in Ecuador 5,300 years ago to its highest apex in the cultures of Mesoamerica.

Chocolate's Apex in Mesoamerica

THE HISTORY OF THE IMPORTANCE OF CACAO AND CHOCOLATE TO MESOAMERICA IS vast. From the indigenous root words for cacao and chocolate, to their ceremonial and spiritual significance, and to the economic power of cacao, it's clear how the cultures of Mesoamerican cultivated, processed, profited from and revered cacao. Based on the remaining indigenous codices that artfully depict chocolate ceremonies, the sixteenth-century Spanish chronicles that attempt to explain the New World wonders to the Old World, and the extensive research conducted by scholars, there are very few stones unturned about the significance of cacao and chocolate in Mesoamerica. In fact, one could spend a lifetime studying the volumes available on the subject—and on the ongoing scholarship and modern scientific analysis that continue to further this knowledge.

Nonetheless, throughout my decades of travels worldwide, and specifically in Central America, I've kept a very close eye on any nugget of new chocolate information; I've tried to sniff out some unique and unusual tidbits from the world of chocolate that only the serendipity of travel can present. My travel curiosity extends to aspects of cultural anthropology, including the role of women in religion, their representation in art, and their knowledge of natural healing modalities, as well as related extraordinary customs. For the last five decades, I've spent numerous days tagging along with various local scholars as they shared their knowledge of the Maya culture in various Central American archaeological sites—Chichén Itzá, Tikal, Palenque, Uxmal, Calakmul, Ek Balam, Cobá, and Tulum. Many of these sites are now easier to reach, but local authorities have also introduced increasingly restrictive access regulations for the protection of each site, limitations which were nonexistent early on in my travels.

FIG. 23

At these archaeological sites and through further reading, I learned to appreciate the importance of cacao in Mesoamerica in the imagery of cacao pods, blood, and the ballgames in Chiapas and Guatemala. The symbolic connection between a cacao pod and the heart or blood is easily recognizable in a stela that depicts a ballplayer holding a knife in one hand and offering a cacao pod to a deity. In their book *Chocolate Pathways to the Gods*, Meredith Dreiss and Sharon Greenhill suggest that the "cacao pod may have replaced the human heart as an offering because both the heart and the heart-shaped cacao pod served as repositories for precious liquids—blood and chocolate."[19] Self-sacrifice and bloodletting in ancient Mesoamerica, they contend, was performed to guarantee a bountiful cacao crop.[20] To this day, the agriculturists of Comalcalco, Tabasco have a harvest ritual where "thousands of multicolored cacao pods from outlying cacao plantations are lashed to long branches."[21]

To me, these ancient sites spoke volumes. At Chichén Itzá, I climbed to the top of the pyramid— no longer allowed—for a close look at the carved stone Chac Mool, the statue of a reclining male figure with his head turned ninety degrees, a bowl balanced on his stomach. I had read that Maya priests and philosophers, who were admired for their oratory skills, spoke in two-word metaphors that had a third hidden meaning. With a bird's eye view from the peak of the pyramid, I understood the importance of the bowl for sacrificial items—and more importantly, I understood the metaphor. This close to the sky, blood sacrifice was offered to the gods above. The priestly metaphor of "*yollotl, eztli*"—heart, blood—was a figure of speech for chocolate, and also signified that the heart and the blood are to be feared.[22]

FIG. 24

My profession as a marriage and family therapist prepared me to extend empathy and understanding to people from different cultures. But it was my second profession as a writer of historical fiction that propelled me to experience the life of my subjects—to feel what my characters might feel, and to ask the really unusual questions. Forty years ago, in order to write about the smallest woman who ever lived for my book *Lucía Zárate,* I pushed my physical limits by climbing the then-rickety ladders of the Guatemalan Maya site of Tikal just to feel very small, weak, and unsure of my steps. I also took a moonless walk in the rainforest of the Palenque archaeological site, in deathly fear, to listen to the roar of a jaguar in his natural habitat—just so I could write with authenticity.

My nugget of travel serendipity, uncovering new chocolate information, occurred in the southern state of Chiapas, Mexico, when a group of armed Maya Zapatista activists forcibly stopped our vehicle on a road near San Cristobal de Las Casas. The Zapatista Movement of 1994, fighting for indigenous rights, continues to this day, but back then both activists and civilians might be killed. They made us follow them down an overgrown ravine to a clearing below the road. I sat quietly on a log for several hours while machete-toting young indigenous women, wearing bandana masks, lectured me on the demands for justice written in their communiqué.

These young Maya women, dressed in their traditional white flowered-embroidered tops and full woven skirts, looked charming and innocent, but in their determined gazes, I knew I'd better not budge from the log or ask any questions. I'd seen that same fierceness, that feral determination, in those who've been forced into subservience in many parts of the world. Eventually, I was al-

FIG. 25

lowed to drink from my water bottle and I unwrapped a melting chocolate bar from my handbag. At first, the two young Zapatista women nearest me declined to share my chocolate bar, but eventually they couldn't resist the aroma of the dark chocolate I prefer. They lifted the bottom triangle of their bandanas and chomped on the chocolate bar.

I told them about my vacations as a child in the cacao plantation in Ecuador, but I didn't say a word about the hacienda belonging to my grandfather, nor did I mention the bloody machete that had scared Federico to death: it was eerily similar to the ones the Zapatistas were wielding. Soon the Zapatistas were bragging, in Spanish, that the original chocolate in the "whole world is from Maya cacao that has always grown near the coast in Chiapas." I joined their boisterous cheers of "*Viva Chiapas!*"

In that instant of exhilaration, I recognized that chocolate was their proud patrimony—or rather, their intrinsic maternal heritage, since it has always been women who cultivated the cacao and then laboriously turned it into chocolate. Their cheers were testimony to the Zapatista's veneration of the bitter water or *xocolatl*/chocolate that was a vital part of Maya identity, and has historically played a significant role in their rituals, economic, and political life.

These proud and resolute Zapatista women were not quite correct. Chocolate did not begin with the Maya. Scientists can now prove that the origins of

FIG. 26

cacao in Mesoamerica did not begin with the Olmecs, either. Olmec culture is remembered for the Colossal Heads, each carved from a single basalt boulder and weighing many tons, believed to represent their dynastic rulers. The Olmecs were once credited as the originators of chocolate, but have been displaced by the culture of the Soconusco region of the Pacific Coast of Mexico and Guatemala, where the best *criollo* cacao was cultivated.[23]

Like the Olmecs, this culture spoke a Mixe-Zoquean language, and preceded the Maya. In *The True History of Chocolate*, Sophie and Michael Coe support the theory of the spread of cacao from Ecuador via coastal trade routes "into the Soconusco region, where some innovator discovered by 1800 BC the complex method of converting seed into chocolate."[24]

The Olmec culture (1600 BCE to 350 BCE) may have used the word *kakawa*/cacao from the Mixe-Zoquean culture, which was then adopted by "emerging cultures elsewhere in Mesoamerica, including the Maya.[25] However, it is the Maya who are credited with the word *kakaw*. Cacao, along with maize, are described in the *Popol Vuh* or the Book of Counsel, the sacred Maya creation narrative,

FIG. 27

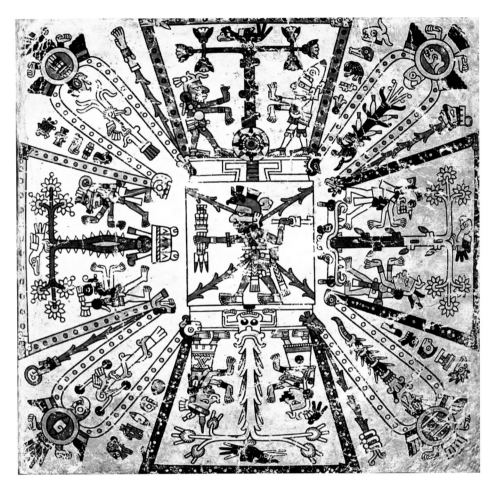

FIG. 28

as the precious substances from which humans are made.[26] Throughout their long history, the Maya also developed hieroglyphic writing on *kopó,* fig tree bark. These codices were folded accordion-style. The Spanish clerics thought them idolatrous and burned most of them, but from the remaining codices we can see how cacao is depicted and its importance to the culture. In the Dresden Codex— so called because it is held in the Royal Library of Dresden—we learn that cacao is the food of the Opossum God. In the Madrid Codex, four gods are depicted as piercing their own ears and "scattering showers of precious blood over the cacao pods."[27] This codex also depicts a woman letting blood from her tongue.[28]

Subsequent Mesoamerican cultures would continue to promulgate the association of chocolate with blood. In the Codex Féjévary-Mayer, an Aztec manuscript, the cacao tree represents the Tree of the South, and thus the Land of the Dead, an artistic record of cacao's association with both death and blood.[29]

In the various eras and regions of Mesoamerica, cacao was held in reverence for its divine properties, and was ritually consumed as a chocolate drink during religious events. Chocolate was associated with high status and with special

FIG. 29

occasions. The first depiction of the chocolate beverage is not evident in any of the extant codices, but it is prominent in the Princeton Vase, a late Classic Maya (circa 750 CE) chocolate-drinking cup. The Princeton Vase portrays a narrative that revolves around the vase, a mythological story that celebrates the cunning of certain heroic figures.[30] The scene illustrates God L, ruler of the underworld, the Maya patron deity of tobacco and merchants. God L is surrounded by five elegant women, one of whom is serving chocolate.

A standing woman with her head bent in concentration suggests that the viewer rotate the vase to the left. She holds a vessel similar in size and shape to the Princeton Vase, and a stream of liquid pours down from it, presumably into a vessel whose rendering has eroded. This method of preparation likely frothed the bitter chocolate beverage that this vessel was made to serve.[31]

The three women behind God L are having a lively conversation while "one pours liquid from a vase; it has been assumed that she is frothing chocolate by pouring it from one container to another."[32]

The classic Mesoamerican chocolate drink was bitter and finely ground, combining cacao and water. It could be reddened by adding achiote, made spicy with chili peppers or sweetened with wild honey. Another enhancement could be aromatic tropical flowers in powder form, like *tlilxochitl* (vanilla).[33] *Teonacaztli* (divine ear), sometimes called *xochinacaztli* (flowery ear) or *hueinacaztli* (great ear), is the flower petal of the tree *Cymbopetalum penduliflorum*. It was renowned for its aromatic spice fragrance, and "was the premier chocolate flavor among the Aztecs."[34]

As depicted in the Princeton Vase, the methodical steps in creating the crucial edible foam were vital in the high-status chocolate-beverage ceremony. Mesoamerican cultures, such as the Zapotec, revered the wind or breath or spirit called pè: this was "the vital force that made all living things move. Anything that moved was thus alive, to some degree sacred, and deserving of respect."[35] To create the foam on top of the cup chocolate, the women who prepared it poured from one vase to another or from a spouted vessel to a vase, thereby creating movement, animating the foam, and paying homage to pè.

The Tudela Codex depicts a Mesoamerican woman wearing a huipil (woven tunic) who pours chocolate from a vessel held at shoulder-height to another on

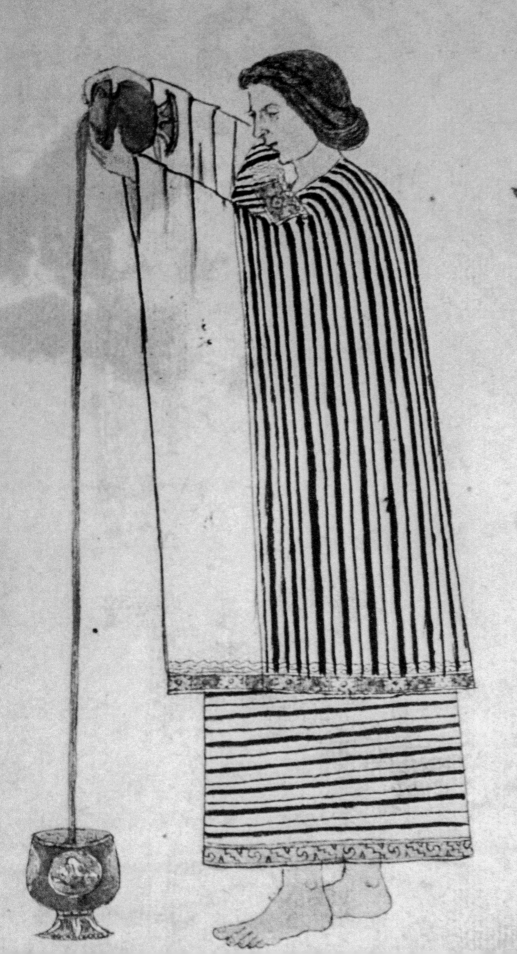

FIG. 31

the floor, in order to create foam. This was labor and time-intensive for the women, but was a revered process since it was symbolic of vitality and life. "In Nahua metaphors, clothes and food represented vitality, and thus women, as producer of these goods provided life's basic necessities."[36]

Cacao and chocolate played an important role in the marriage traditions of Mesoamerica. The Codex Zouche-Nuttall, held in the British Museum, depicts an exchange of cacao beans during a Mixtec marriage ceremony. In the Florentine Codex, "noble parents inform their daughter that it will be her womanly duty *(mociotequiuh)* to prepare food and beverages."[37] Even today, folklore in the region maintains that "chocolate is for the body, but the foam is for the soul."[38] In fact, in present-day Central America, chocolate is imbued with religious meaning and is consumed at religious festivities such as weddings and baptisms. During the marriage ceremony, known as *quicyuj* by the Maya of Guatemala, cacao beans remain a part of the dowry and marriage contract.

We can admire the elegant women who poured chocolate, as depicted in the Princeton Vase and the Tudela Codex, but it's hard to imagine the tremendous effort made to turn bitter seeds into a drink for the gods. The women who cultivate cacao have always known that after harvesting and opening the cacao pods, the hard work has just begun. Each pod contains around four dozen seeds that must be removed. During the five-to-seven day fermentation period, the seeds excrete liquid and exude aromas. Cacao seeds, also known as beans, are dried in the sun for one week and raked continuously to ensure even drying. These dried beans can be stored in the proper environment for up to five years. The beans are then roasted to bring out the flavors. During the winnowing process, the fibrous husk is removed. In the Mesoamerican tradition, the remaining nibs of cacao are then ground with a stone roller on the surface of a *metate* or grindstone with a hot brazier beneath. The resulting spread will be a paste of cacao butter and cacao solids. Despite all the labor put into the preparation of the chocolate beverage, women were not allowed to drink it.[39]

The women who prepared the beverage also had considerable knowledge of the medicinal benefits of chocolate. The addition of string flower, *mecaxóchitl,* not only added a peppery flavor, but helped relieve stomach pains and colics.[40] A drink made with the flower and seeds of heart flower—*yolloxochitl* or *Magnolia Mexicana*—was "supposed to augment the pulse and regularize the heartbeat," although an overdose could cause arrythmia.[41]

According to the gendered division of labor in Mesoamerica in various eras, women wove textiles, prepared food and beverages, and practiced various degrees of healing. But as a result of their dedication to the cultivation and preparation of cacao, they also became involved in the economic arena as traders of this luxury item.

The Codex Zouche-Nuttall

The pictographs and glyphs of the Codex Zouche-Nuttall reveal that the Mixtec ruler Lord Eight Deer (1063 CE–1115 CE)—known as "Jaguar Claw"— controlled alliances between the cacao-growing regions stretching inland from coastal Oaxaca. At the age of just eighteen, Lord Eight Deer had the ambition and the determination to "take advantage of the ecological verticality of a highlands-to-coastal corridor."[42] His ascent as conqueror is depicted on pages 50 and 51 of the codex, defeating Tututepec on the coast, and Tilantongo in the highlands.[43]

I've had a particular interest in the Codex Zouche-Nuttall for two reasons. First, Lord Eight Deer's climb to power reads like a heroic novel, and I'm a voracious reader of such stories. When he was seventeen, he realized he would not inherit a title, so he and his followers traveled to the coast of Oaxaca: after a violent campaign, they took control of the trade in luxury items like cacao, feathers, salt, and cotton. En route, Lord Eight Deer Jaguar Claw performed sacrifices, confronted adversaries in a cave and men in Toltec costume on a ballcourt, and—most significantly—met with the oracle Lady Nine Grass, who forecasted fame and fortune for him.[44]

Once he conquered the coastal polity of Tututepec and wrested control of their luxury-goods trade, he was seen as an attractive alliance partner for highland nobles. Eventually, Lord Eight Deer became the lord of Tilantongo—in the Oaxacan highlands, approximately 500 miles from the coast—without having any blood ties to the title.

The Codex Zouche-Nuttall depicts the genealogy of Lord Eight Deer, including the marriage of his father, Lord Five Crocodile, to Lady Nine Eagle, who was called Garland of Cacao Flowers. The cultural significance of cacao and chocolate in trade, and in the subsequent marriage of Lord Eight Deer to

FIG. 32

the Lady Thirteen Serpent, is emphasized in the prominence given to the frothy chocolate drink served at their marriage and at other significant ceremonies.

In 2005 I discovered the history of Lord Eight Deer when I attended a wedding held at the archaeological site of Monte Albán, Mexico, approximately 105 miles from Lord Eight Deer Jaguar Claw's capital of Tilantongo. For well over one thousand years, Monte Albán was a powerful city in Mesoamerica, founded in the sixth century BCE, first inhabited by the Zapotec and then the Mixtec civilizations. The Monte Albán site was severely damaged in the 2017 earthquake.

Unlike the ritual-laden marriage of Lord Eight Deer in 1085 CE, the Monte Albán wedding I attended was replete with New Age mystical symbolism that was romantically whimsical. The bride and groom were well into late middle-age, and had invited forty guests to visit Monte Albán and Oaxaca to celebrate the famed *Día de los Muertos*-Day of the Dead festivities: there, at a significant archaeological site, we were surprised with a pop-up wedding. We loved the surprise, especially since we were all still in a celebratory mood. The night before the wedding we all had been up until the wee hours of the morning, after

FIG. 33

participating in a blend of indigenous and Catholic rites in Oaxaca's cemetery, where thousands of candles and burning *copal* incense created a bewitching atmosphere. On the day of the New Age wedding, we all exhibited a joyous
esprit de corps; we sang ballads and recited poetry, given as our spontaneous gifts
to the bride and groom. Later that day at dinner, we feasted on dark chocolate
prepared in the savory Oaxacan *mole negro* sauce that is composed with over
thirty ingredients.

What we did not do at that wedding was dance. Perhaps it was a collective reaction to the low relief stone sculptures we had seen in Monte Albán.
These stone carvings are known as *Los Danzantes*—the dancers—and depict
conquered male victims, naked and in various poses of torture and mutilation.
In ancient Mesoamerica, dancing—and the consumption of the frothy chocolate
beverage—frequently preceded human sacrifice.[45]

The second reason for my fascination with the Codex Zouche-Nuttall is
due to its namesake: Zelia María Magdalena Nuttall. An extraordinary scholar,
linguist, archaeologist and professor, Nuttall pioneered the scholarship on Mesoamerica cultures at the turn of the twentieth century. In 1897 she published an
article called "Ancient Mexican Superstitions" in *the Journal of American Folklore*.
Nuttall questioned the popular belief that ancient Mexicans were "ugly, dwarfish
and bloodthirsty savages, having nothing in common with civilized humanity."[46]

Zelia Nuttall was born in San Francisco, California in 1857 to a Mexican mother and an Irish father. Both parents came from wealthy backgrounds and were able to give her a fine education. The Nuttalls traveled widely, and the family spent extended periods living in England, France Germany and Switzerland. Because of this, and the private tutors who educated her, Zelia developed strong linguistic knowledge and skills. The road she took to becoming an expert in Mesoamerican cultures was a circuitous one. In 1876, she returned to San Francisco from Europe. Four years later she met and married Alphonse Louis Pinart, a French scholar, linguist, ethnologist, explorer and collector. The *San Francisco Chronicle* declared their wedding the social event of the season. The guests were a very select group, and the decorations and dinner were masterpieces.[47] Nuttall traveled extensively with her husband through Europe and to the West Indies. But they separated after four years, divorcing in 1888. Nuttall reclaimed her maiden name and won custody of their young daughter, Nadine.[48] She began her own work as an archaeologist.

On a visit to Teotihuacán, Mexico, Nuttall collected several terracotta heads that, she contended, were created by the Aztecs near the time of the Spanish Conquest, although they were not all made in the same location. She concluded that these heads were once attached to bodies made from degradable materials, and that the figures were portraits of individuals representing the dead. Nuttall published her results in *The American Journal of Archaeology and the History of the Fine Arts* in 1886, and her research was well received.[49]

Nuttall continued her independent research and published other works—notably, *The Fundamental Principles of Old and New World Civilizations*. She was appointed a special assistant in Mexican archaeology at Harvard's Peabody Museum. On August 16, 1892, *The Boston Evening Transcript* wrote: "on all matters relating to Mexican history she is an authority. Two of the Peabody Museum monographs are by her."[50]

Nuttall's most lasting contribution to archaeology is her research and translation of the codex that bears her name. Like Nuttall's own circuitous journey into archaeology, the Zouche-Nuttall Codex—made from animal skin, and folded accordion-style—traveled from Mexico to Spain in the sixteenth century. Nuttall learned about its existence from a historian at the Monastery of San Marco in Florence.[51] In 1859 the codex ended up in the collection of Robert Curzon, 14th Baron Zouche of Haynworth, England. Zelia Nuttall and the Peabody Museum of Archaeology and Ethnology were able to translate the codex and

FIG. 35

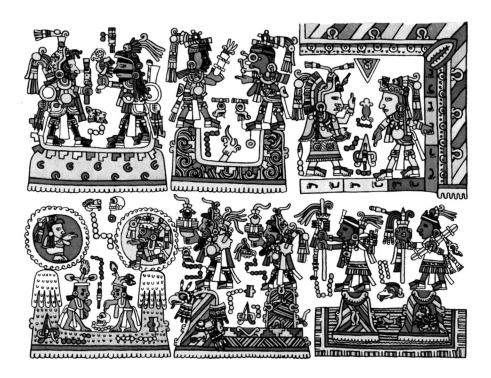

FIG. 36

publish a facsimile in 1902.[52] "To her great joy, the codex was not only perfect and intact in every part, but the wooden covers, enveloped in deerskin, looked as fresh as though they had been put on only 20 years before, and the contents, the colors of the hieroglyphs and picture-writing were as bright as the day they were put on."[53]

The genealogy of the Mixtec Lord Eight Deer Jaguar Claw features prominently in the Codex Zouche-Nuttall. From images in the codex, we learn how determined he was to control trade of the coastal resources of Oaxaca, including cacao, cotton, feathers, fish and salt.[54] We also see his strategic alliances with the men and women of the *pochteca* merchant class, depicted in the codex with staves and fans: they traded in the luxury goods Lord Eight Deer Jaguar Claw so coveted. The codex also shows the murder of his older half-brother, 12 Movement, and makes clear that the ritual offering at the funeral is chocolate.

Mesoamerican Women
Traders and *Cacicas*

*I*T'S A PITY THAT ZELIA NUTTALL'S SCHOLARLY INTEREST DIDN'T FOCUS ON THE women who participated as traders in the Aztec economy. Her in-depth study and interpretation of the indigenous codices would have revealed the degree of trade involvement by the women cacao producers, chocolate preparers and ritual servers. After all, Nuttall was a scholar who was interested and committed to the revival of Mexican traditions that had been eradicated by Spanish conquest.[55] In 1928, she advocated the renewal of celebrating the Aztec New Year, the day when "the sun reached its zenith and cast no shadows."[56] On December 12, 1928, *The Kansas City Star* wrote:

> After a lapse of four centuries the Feast of the Sun, considered one of the most beautiful ceremonies known to the ancient civilization, has been restored to its place in the national life of Mexico by an American woman, Mrs. Zelia Nuttall, famous archaeologist.[57]

Inevitably, after living and studying in Mexico for decades, Nuttall would have encountered the ubiquitous women market sellers, these enterprising descendants of the Mesoamerican women who were the backbone of ancient commerce. And, most assuredly, Nuttall would have heard the legend of the Oaxacan Zapotec princess Donají.

Donají lived in pre-Columbian Oaxaca, probably born in the late fifteenth century. As a result of a broken peace treaty, the Mixtecs held Donají captive in Monte Albán. When the Zapotecs broke the treaty and attacked Monte Albán, the remaining Mixtecs retaliated, beheading Donají. Not only does Donají's image still grace the official seal of the city of Oaxaca, but her fiery spirit is evident in the famously independent, brash, and economically astute women who still

FIG. 37

dominate the regional trade centers of Tehuantepec and Juchitán in Oaxaca. It has been a pleasure, and a lesson well-learned, to negotiate with these quick-witted and forceful women vendors, be it for their exquisite hand-loomed or hand-embroidered clothing or eighteen-karat gold jewelry. They've outmaneuvered me at every transaction. Ever since the sixteenth century, foreign chroniclers have remarked on these market women, dubbed Tehuanas, since they hailed from the regional market city of Tehuantepec in Oaxaca. The Tehuanas are still legendary for their economic savvy, cocksure character, and flamboyant native dress, made famous by the iconic attire of twentieth-century Mexican artist Frida Kahlo.

The Aztec economy was based on three things: agricultural goods, tribute, and trade. In trade, the three categories of commercial practitioners were: "the household producer-seller (*tlachiuhhqui*), the general merchandiser and market vender (*tlanamacac*), and the commercial retailer (*tlanecuilo*).[58] Mesoamerican commerce operated in local, regional, and main marketplaces. It is interesting to note that women were involved in all the economic aspects of the high-value products such as plain and embroidered textiles.[59] Women were the dyers, spinners, weavers and vendors of textiles.

Without question the marketplace had important social and political functions. After all, the marketplace was where people socialized, news was spread,

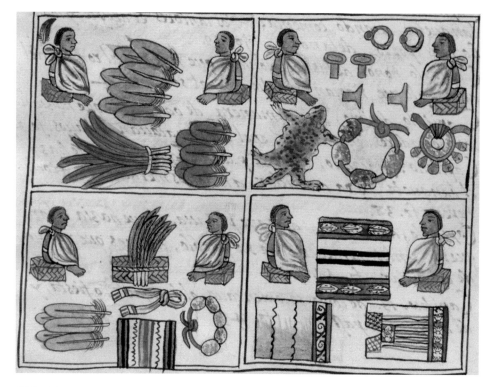

FIG. 38

and where foreign spies could assess both the power and sentiment of the people toward their rulers.

By 1473 CE, the Aztecs of Tenochtitlan had used military might to expand their long-distance trade in luxury goods. Their highly efficient trade system was known as *pochteca*, which means "People from the Land of the Ceiba-tree" or the tropical lowlands.[60] This trade system was made up of four groups: slave traders; disguised or spy merchants; general merchants, and the royal travelers, also known as the vanguard traders.[61] Through their trade of luxury items such as quetzal feathers, jaguar skins, amber, and cacao, the vanguard traders grew very wealthy. The human caravans of vanguard traders were highly regulated due to value of their cargo, as well as the restrictions imposed by sumptuary laws about dress and the consumption of chocolate, which was for the elite class only.

Book Nine of the Florentine Codex, compiled circa 1542, describes the function and rituals of the Aztec *pochteca*. When the vanguard merchants presented their offerings before they set out to trade, chocolate was served and drunk. Once they returned from their trading journey, they held an all-night banquet where chocolate was drunk before ingesting hallucinogenic mushrooms and honey.[62] Once the individual hallucinations were analyzed, by the group, the traders believed in the destiny foretold during their visions:

FIG. 39

That one would take captives, one would become a seasoned warrior, one would die in battle, become rich, buy slaves, commit adultery, be strangled, perish in the water, drown. Whatsoever was to befall one, they then saw all [in vision].[63]

Throughout Book 9, the discussion of the merchant class almost always refers to male merchants. A mention of merchant women appears in the sixth chapter of the Florentine Codex, which tells how the merchants prepared before making offerings: "When they had assembled—indeed everyone, the kinsmen and the merchant women, those who ceremoniously bathed slaves—thereupon hands were washed, [and] mouths were washed."[64] However, women did not generally participate in long-distance trade journeys.[65] As producers and craftswomen, women traveled together or with a group of men on shorter distances to sell their goods.[66] On one occasion Aztec women on their way to market at Coyoacán with their merchandise were robbed of everything they carried, then raped.[67]

Despite the assaults endured by Aztec women vendors, they continued to trade in the marketplace.[68] It was customary for traders to pay homage at various crossroad shrines. These *cihuapipiltin* were dedicated to the dangerous spirits of women who had died at childbirth.[69] With the hazards the women vendors faced on their road trips, they must have hoped that their reverence at the shrines would give them protection.

Although mentions of women traders in the Florentine Codex are few, it is evident that the women traders among the *pochteca* had specific duties to perform. The traders gave gifts to all the women who bathed the slaves. These gifts were skirts, shifts, and feather pendants.[70] The ceremonial women bathers, in return, gave the female slaves gifts of shifts and skirts, and pasted feathers on the slaves.

The existence of merchant women among the *pochteca* is cited again in the Eighth Chapter of the Florentine Codex, describing a type of group confession that took place among the merchants. The male merchants are prodded by the guild leader into remembering their past transgressions: "Perhaps thou hast filched some woman's belongings: her goods. Thou hast robbed someone."[71] Whatever goods the women traders had in their possession must have been valuable enough to provoke envy, and the theft of said items must have occurred with such frequency that the leading merchant felt the need to chastise the male traders.

The Spanish chroniclers translated the native codices and described the local customs, revealing the complexity of the regional markets and the great marketplace of Tlatelolco, where "virtually every kind of good available in the empire could be found."[72] According to the sources, there were one hundred and twenty four types of producer-seller that produced most of the "food, fiber, and craft goods consumed in Mesoamerica."[73] Fray Toribio de Motolinía wrote that "at these markets, called *tianquiztli* by the Indians, they sell whatever is found in this land, from gold and silver to reeds and firewood."[74] Even Cortés noted that 60,000 buyers and sellers congregated daily in the Tlatelolco market, located in the Aztec capital of Tenochtitlan, south east of the Templo Mayor.[75]

Around 1581, Fray Diego Durán wrote:

> The markets were so inviting, pleasurable, appealing, and gratifying to these people that great crowds attended, and still attend them, especially during the big feasts, as is well known to all. I suspect that if I said to a market woman accustomed to going from market to market: 'Look, today is market day in such and such a town. What would you rather do, go from here right to Heaven or go to that market?' I believe this would be her answer: 'Allow me to go to that market first, and then I will go to Heaven.[76]

These great Mesoamerican markets were composed of a two-way system of full-time professional craftspeople and specialists; the highly structured *pochteca* guilds; the tribute goods that moved one way, from producers to elite consumer; and the local producers and vendors.[77]

The Codex Mendoza lists the massive amount of cacao tribute paid to the Aztec king Moctezuma. Chiapas paid four hundred loads of cacao, each load weighing fifty pounds and hauled on the backs of human cargo carriers. The annual tribute of cacao to the Aztec ruler was twenty tons.[78] Local producers of cacao, cotton, and salt often transported their own products to market.

Since women were the producers of cacao, it is probable that they also traveled to market with their products. However, luxury products like cacao were generally part of the full-time merchant system.

Women were important traders in the marketplace. The Spanish chronicles indicate that "women were closely associated with market activities such as food venders of maize, beans, chia, amaranth, gourd seeds, fruit and prepared foods including chocolate."[79] The Aztec markets were rigidly administered and controlled. Everyone who entered the market paid a tax in service or goods, and a rent was charged for a place at the market.[80] Barter was the primary means of exchange in the market places.[81] Additionally, cloth and cacao beans served as currency. "The three cacao varieties regularly used for currency were *cacahuatl*, *mecacahuatl*, and *xochicachuatl*, while the small bean variety (*tlalcacahuatl*) was more often used for drinks."[82]

The market directors were often women responsible for inspecting goods and for setting price ceilings on the goods for sale.[83] The market directors held a position of respect and were selected for their past experience, so older women engaged in trade often attained this honor and duty.[84] The value of cacao as currency at the markets was controlled. A small rabbit was worth 30 cacao beans. One turkey egg was worth three cacao beans, but one turkey hen was work 100 cacao beans.[85] All market administrators had to be on alert for deceitful selling practices. Since cacao was used as currency, it was often counterfeited by removing the shell of the cacao bean and filling it with dirt. The counterfeiter also removed the valuable cacao nib which was then sold or used to make chocolate.[86]

The markets had an enormous variety of goods for sale, including feathers, jade, food, shoes, stones, metals, chocolate and vanilla, tools, slaves, clothes, and pottery. The rules of behavior were strictly monitored, and any deviation from the assigned role was punished. The roles of each type of seller were clearly defined and given a name. Cacao vendors were known as the *cacaonamacac*, and chocolate sellers were called *tlaquetzalnamacac*. It's been noted that in the Florentine Codex, nine out of twenty types of producer-traders are women. There are errors in the Spanish chronicles where the fruit sellers are defined as masculine, but the pictographs reveal that the fruit vendors were women. These sellers also made sweets with the fruit, chia and squash products.[87]

The Spanish chronicler Bernal Díaz del Castillo's amazement at the market of Tlatelolco is evident in his book *The True History of the Conquest of Mexico*, completed in 1572:

> When we arrived at the market in the large plaza, Tlatelolco, as we had
> not seen such a thing, we were astonished at the multitude of people
> and quantity of merchandize and at the good order and control they
> had everywhere. The chieftains who were with us went along showing

FIG. 40

it to us. Each type of merchandise was by itself and had its place fixed
and marked out.[88]

Three-hundred-and-fifty years later, in 1935, the renowned twentieth-
century muralist Diego Rivera completed his famous mural *El Tianguis de Tlatelolco* (The Marketplace at Tlatelolco) at the National Palace in Mexico City. He
spent years researching the writings of Bernal Díaz del Castillo, as well as studying the native codices, and then amalgamated them with his own knowledge of
the visual feast that are the Mexican open-air markets.

The market mural is just a section of a much larger series of murals painted
on the walls of the *Palacio Nacional*. The lower center of the *Tianguis de Tlatelolco*
mural depicts the panoply of vendors, products for sale, and the energy of the
exchange, specifically the trade of cacao. Throughout the mural, there are images
of women vendors selling their respective products. At the center of the mural,
two women are depicted in the midst of an economic exchange. One is selling
maize and the other one is paying with cacao beans.

The wealth amassed by the indigenous women producers and sellers of
cacao and other luxury items is evident in the colonial records of the sixteenth
century. They indicate that women owned individual land holdings known as
cihuatlalli.[89] Women *cacicas*—female hereditary chiefs or noblewomen—often became embroiled in lawsuits pertaining their estates. The *cacicas* fought to "protect
their rights and privileges, and through these cases and the special awards, permits
and protections granted by the Spanish Crown officials, we know a great deal
about certain royal women in the Mixteca."[90]

Through the colonial proceedings of María Rojas, the cacica of Chica-
huastla, we learn that she paid tribute to the Spanish governor and to the local

Spanish officials. At the same time she received tributes from commoners—primarily luxury items such as cotton cloth, cacao, turkeys, salt, and pine torches.[91]

Ana Sosa was the *cacica* from the coastal region in the province of Tututepec. This is the same cacao-producing region that the Mixtec Lord Eight Deer Jaguar Claw once fought to claim as his territory. In 1522 the Spanish conqueror Pedro de Alvarado fought fierce battles with the Mixtecs because both sides acknowledged that Tututepec was a very rich area.[92] Pedro de Alvarado is considered the most depraved, cruel and avaricious among the Spanish invaders.[93]

Ana Sosa's land holdings exceeded those of the most powerful Spanish land grantee in the region, and it is estimated that only the estate of Hernán de Cortés in the Valley of Oaxaca would have exceeded hers.[94] "Mexica cacicas were equal in rank to their brothers and husbands and succeeded to titles in their own right."[95] Ana Sosa possessed:

> Twelve estancias; thirty-one groves of cacao; great stretches of farming and grazing lands, highly productive saltworks; lagoons rich in fish, game and shellfish; and numerous houses, including the palace complex in Tututepec. She also held valuable movable property in the form of gold, silver, jade, coral, and turquoise jewelry, precious bird plumage, vast quantities of cotton huipiles (blouses) and skirts and other textiles, livestock, and stores of products from her fields and other resources.[96]

Documented in the 1580 will of the eighty-one-year-old Angelina Martina, a market administrator at Tlatelolco, is a summary of the wealth she amassed as a stationary merchant of the *pochteca*.[97] She left twenty-one properties, several agricultural lands, storage facilities and loans due to her. Her wealth was a result of her specialization in the craft and commerce of exotic feather work for plumed garments, headdresses, shields and images.[98] The Spanish admired the crafted plumed work and shipped them back to Spain to use on clerical attire. Angelina Martina's will does not mention a husband and all her properties were in her name alone. She left all her estate to her grandchildren and great-grandchildren.

By the end of Angeline Martina's life, the Spanish had taken control over the sale of products and the viceroy had appropriated the role of the *pochteca*. "The policies and practices of the Spanish authorities contributed to the slow erosion in women's status over time."[99] The only vestiges remaining of the powerful *cacicas* are their large but dilapidated houses, known by local inhabitants as *Casa de la Cacica*.

The Chocolate Wind

THE MAGIC OF TRAVEL SERENDIPITY STRUCK AGAIN IN 2007 WHEN I RECEIVED A very rare invitation by the then-owners of an historic house. This had once belonged to the most maligned and misunderstood woman in Mexican history, known pejoratively as *La Malinche*.

I listened attentively as the owners told me their perspective on *La Malinche*. She was born around 1500, and remembered as the indigenous traitor and mistress of the Spanish invader Hernán Cortés. But in reality, she was a victim of kidnapping, slavery, and rape at the hands of her own family. They sold her to indigenous slave traders, who took a young Malinche from her home in Veracruz to Tabasco. There, in 1519, she was given as a gift to Cortés. It was early in his conquest of Mesoamerica, but he had also received 19 other indigenous maidens as gifts. He gave Malintzin to one of his captains, Alonso Hernández Puertocarrero. But after her linguistic talents and diplomatic skills became apparent to Cortés, he took her back as his interpreter—and mistress.

All chroniclers from the era agree that she was a beautiful and brilliant interpreter, as well as an insightful cultural guide for Cortés. Her birth name remains an enigma, but she was called Malintzin in Nahual, mispronounced as Malinche by the Spanish, and then given the Christian name and honorific title of Doña Marina. In the codices and chronicles of the early days of the conquest, she is always depicted next to Cortés, serving as his relay interpreter from Chontal Maya or Nahual, while Franciscan Friar Jerónimo de Aguilar, who spoke Chontal Maya as a result of having been enslaved by the Maya for eight years, translated her words into Spanish.

Once Doña Marina learned to speak Spanish, she was able to communicate directly with Cortés. She is remembered for her military intelligence, anticipating

an attack by the army of Cholula indigenous warriors against Cortés, thus saving the Spanish forces—and sealing her infamy as a traitor to the indigenous people of Mexico. The Spanish chronicler Bernal Díaz del Castillo wrote of her in glowing terms:

> After Our Lord God, it was she who caused New Spain to be won.
> Without her, we couldn't do anything.
> Without her, we wouldn't have won this land.[100]

Doña Marina's link to the world of chocolate is through her ongoing interpreting relationship with Friar Jerónimo de Aguilar. Both are tragic historical

FIG. 43

FIG. 44

figures, who survived the painful trajectory of their lives during the bloody invasion of Mesoamerica, spurred by the insatiable greed of the Spanish Crown. Both were survivors who traveled with Cortés as part of his skilled entourage, as he expanded the Spanish Empire in the former Mesoamerica. Doña Marina's intimate proximity to Cortés, and her fluency in three languages, along with her poetic interpretation of the Aztec leader, made her invaluable to Cortés. Soon Jerónimo de Aguilar, with his limited linguistic abilities, was not needed. He began rumors to the effect that Doña Marina had "not behaved nobly on all occasions."[101]

After Cortés destroyed the Aztec capital, he went to live in the nearby community of Coyoacán in 1522. It provided fertile and level ground with an abundance of fresh water, and Cortés enjoyed the economic advantage of forcing six thousand households to work for him.[102] Doña Marina lived with him in the palace of the former ruler of Coyoacán. Soon she was pregnant. Cortés' legal wife, Catalina Suarez, arrived with her Spanish entourage, but without any of the children she so badly wanted. Doña Marina raised Martín, her son with Cortés, in a red stucco house that still exists in Coyoacán. The legend of a tunnel that connected her house to the house where Cortés lived with his legal

FIG. 45

wife persists to this day. Catalina Suarez was a jealous wife who was strangled to death by an unknown assailant in the middle of the night in the Cortés house in Coyoacán.[103]

In 2007, when I arrived at the house of *La Malinche* in Coyoacán, the limited light of dusk added an element of trepidation. The exterior walls have been painted blood red ever since she commanded them to be so, but on that evening, the fluctuating shadows on its rough stucco walls seemed to be drenched in coagulated dark blood. I'd heard a litany of legends from artist friends living in Coyoacán for days before my visit, so I already had strong feelings about the humiliation and misfortune endured by Doña Marina in this very house—and I was primed to sense the supernatural melancholy that permeated the interior of the house.

My hosts were both well-known artists from the generation of Mexican artists trained by famed muralist Diego Rivera and Frida Kahlo, and known as *Los Fridos*. I'd met them the night before at the home one of Mexico's finest sculptors. Unlike the lively evening at his home, my visit to the house of *La Malinche* was somber. My hosts, both octogenarians, shuffled from one dim room to the other, and pointed out the location of the supposed tunnel which allowed Cortés to visit Doña Marina in secret.

Despite their impeccable manners, my hosts no longer wanted to talk about Frida Kahlo's deeply felt Mexican nationalism that pervaded her art when she lived a few blocks away in her famous cobalt-blue house.[104] They could only muster a few words about the archaeologist Zelia Nuttall's residence, known as *Casa de Alvarado*, once the home of the most heinous conquistador Pedro de Alvarado, and just a short walking distance away. Nonetheless, the once vivacious and artistically accomplished *Los Fridos* did manage to recite a partial stanza from Nobel Poet Octavio Paz, who had coincidentally died in the *de Alvarado* house in Coyoacán in 1998:

> I opened my eyes late.
> For a second of a second
> I felt what the Aztec felt,
> on the crest of the promontory,
> lying in wait …

Their voices faded off and the last word of the stanza drifted away. On cue, their servant unceremoniously plopped a cup of thick hot chocolate in front of me, along with a stale roll that stuck in my throat. We swirled the bread in the chunky chocolate, but we didn't drink it. The mood was pensive. The spark of the lively night before had died out. All that was left in their gloomy salon were

FIG. 46

the barely visible outlines of their artworks and the floating shadows of the misery that had been *Malintzin, La Malinche,* Doña Marina's life.

❋ ❋ ❋

Her former fellow interpreter Jerónimo de Aguilar (1489-1531) is often—and erroneously—credited with being the first Spaniard to send back cacao beans from Mexico. He is said to have sent them around 1530 to the monastery of La Piedra in the mountainous north of Spain, where cacao supposedly remained a secret for many years. Like many legends, this one has many holes. It is most unlikely that Friar de Aguilar sent cacao to the Abbot of La Piedra: he was a Franciscan friar from Seville in the south of Spain, and would have had little connection with the austere and cloistered Cistercians at the inaccessible Monastery of La Piedra in northeastern Spain. Furthermore, Friar de Aguilar never returned to Spain. He did not live in the port of Veracruz from where the ships sailed, and he died in Mexico.

Christopher Columbus is also thought, erroneously, to have brought the cacao seeds back to Spain. In fact, he did not see any cacao beans until his fourth voyage in 1502, when he captured a Maya trading canoe off the island of Ganaja, near the Honduras coast. In 1503, his son Ferdinand Columbus wrote about this event:

> For their provisions they had such roots and grains as are eaten in
> Hispaniola, and a sort of wine made out of maize which resembled

English beer; and many of those almonds [cacao seeds] which in New Spain [Mexico] are used for money. They seemed to hold these almonds at a great price; for when they were brought on board ship together with their goods, I observed that when any of these almonds fell, they all scooped to pick it up, as if an eye had fallen.[105]

It is also unlikely that Hernán Cortés carried cacao among the luxurious goods he took back to Spain. The Spanish Crown demanded an exact account of all the goods shipped back from the New World since it received its royal fifth on all the goods. In Cortés' detailed inventory of impressive items, such as his inhumane cargo of indigenous men, plus live jaguars, gold, silver, precious stones, exotic feathers, and even armadillos, there is no mention of cacao whatsoever. Although Cortés recognized the importance of cacao seeds as currency among the Mesoamerican cultures, cacao's worth as currency was not transferable to the Spanish Empire, which valued gold and silver. It is also known that in the early years of the Spanish conquest of Mesoamerica, the Spanish were repelled by the taste of the indigenous chocolate drink.

It is more likely that it was the Dominican friar Bartolomé de las Casas (1484-1566) or a member of his influential trading family, who took the cacao beans back to Spain. Starting in 1502, he is known to have made sixteen trans-Atlantic crossings. His father was a well-known trader from an old Seville family who sailed on the second voyage of Christopher Columbus. The de las Casas family owned agricultural land and enslaved indigenous workers in Hispaniola. His father also brought back an indigenous Taino boy, whom he named Juanico, and who became the lifelong servant of Bartolomé de las Casas. If his father, a wily merchant with connections at the port, could manage to return to Seville with a human being, it is very likely that bringing benign contraband like cacao would be an easy feat.

Bartolomé de las Casas dedicated the rest of his long life to fight slavery and denounced the abuse of the indigenous people of the Americas. He eventually became Bishop of Chiapas and made yet another voyage back to Spain. What we know for certain is that in 1544, when de las Casas visited Prince Phillip—soon to be King Philip II—he also brought a group of Maya

FIG. 47

FIG. 48

men, and a long list of unique flora and fauna from Guatemala. His detailed inventory included cacao beans. It is very probable that he left some of the cacao beans in the ancient Dominican monastery of *Porta Coeli* in Seville since this convent had hosted him and dozens of his fellow Dominicans, on many occasions, when they prepared for their long journeys to and from the New World.

The first Spanish chroniclers found the Mesoamerican-style chocolate beverage offensive. Gonzalo Fernández de Oviedo detested the indigenous people almost as much as he hated Bartolomé de las Casas, because de las Casas advocated for a reformed and humane treatment of the locals. He found the drink obnoxious.[106] Not only were the preparation and spices repulsive to him, but the blood-red stains the drink left on the lips signified a pagan and barbaric ritual.

By 1544, the stamina-enhancing benefits of chocolate were acknowledged by the Spanish. They also promoted the benefits of consuming it during religious fasting. These benefits of chocolate could have been the stimulus for leaving the cacao beans in the *Convento de Porta Coeli* for the use of the friars. The appreciation for chocolate consumption in Spain took some time and creativity to develop, but its trans-Atlantic trade was already dubbed as *Viento Chocolatero*, the favorable Chocolate Wind that facilitated the Spanish caravels as they departed from the Gulf of Mexico, carrying this culinary treasure back to Spain.

Convents and
Cultural Fusion

THE SPANISH CROWN EXERTED TOTAL CONTROL ON ITS COLONIES IN THE AMERICAS, but I learned early on that, throughout history, political chaos and violence can infiltrate the thick walls and protective armor of elite Roman Catholic convents. As a result of my parents' bitter divorce, I spent several of my primary school years in the 1950s and early 1960s secluded in a fortress convent run by strict disciplinarian Spanish nuns in Quito, Ecuador. I never felt safe.

My former idyllic and pampered life became an austere existence of constant prayer and punitive education in the convent of the Sisters of Mercy. At first, I had difficulty understanding the Castilian lisp of the arrogant and mean-spirited Spanish nuns. At home, my indigenous nannies would speak to me in their sing-song lilt and used sweet diminutive words throughout the day. They never addressed me as *la niña* (the girl) but as *mi niñita preciosita* (my wee precious little girl). At the convent, when I innocently attempted to emulate the nuns' severe lisp, the Mother Superior slapped me across the mouth with enough force to draw blood from my lips. When she discovered that my great-uncle was the Cardinal of Ecuador, she tried to make amends, but by then I knew her true nature, and I maintained my distance. During the frequent Andean earthquakes, the nuns herded us few boarding students into the chapel in the middle of the night to pray for forgiveness, as if we had caused the shift in the earth's tectonic plates.

The convent was located just blocks away from the Presidential Palace. In November 1961, gunfire and Molotov cocktails filled the air during a vicious coup d'état that lasted several days and killed 35 people. We hid in the subterranean theatre for days, and within weeks of the coup d'état, many of the nuns bolted back to Spain.

After their departure, the browbeaten housekeeping novices—all indigenous girls—started to smile again. The cooks no longer prepared codfish in the bland Iberian way, but served us our Andean thick hot stews topped with slices of avocado and crispy pork skin, and we could count on a hot cup of chocolate served with *quimbolitos*—sweet steamed cakes wrapped in achira leaves—every night. Long gone were the harsh lisping tongues, and now our convent hummed with the sounds of pan flutes and the charming Andean courtesy of our mestizo nuns.

When I researched the very first convent school established in 1528 during Spain's colonial rule in Mexico, I was surprised to learn that the women who started the convent school were not nuns who had taken their vows. In fact, the church did not allow any nuns to make the transatlantic voyage until decades later. The founder was Catalina Bustamante Tinoco, from Extremadura, Spain, and recently widowed. She left Santo Domingo (Dominican Republic) with her two daughters and her two sisters-in-law, and—with the permission of the famed Friar Toribio de Benavente—started a school for girls. It was housed in the former Aztec palace in Texcoco, northwest of Mexico City. Catalina Bustamante Tinoco was a member of the Third Order of Saint Francis: these were women

FIG. 49

who could not take the vows, but who committed themselves to live according to the example of St. Francis of Assisi, by the ideals of poverty and charity.

By the time Catalina started the convent school, the Spanish Crown had imposed its control of every economic, social, and religious facet in the Americas,[107] from exports of gold and silver to which religious orders were permitted to cross the Atlantic. During the colonial era, cacao production increased due both to local indigenous demand and to the increased levels of cacao tribute required by the Spanish Crown. At the religious and fiscal levels, the Crown imposed a tithe on all fruits of the earth, including grain, cotton, sugar, silk, flax, cacao, livestock and dairy products.[108]

Socially, the exchange of culture took place in the intimate realm of home and hearth. The colonial Spanish men of that era either married indigenous women or took them as their mistresses, and increased the magnitude of influence that "Indian wives [had] in acculturating Spanish men (and creating culturally mestizo households) to Indian dietary and domestic practices."[109] As a consequence, the men learned to drink chocolate and appreciated its stamina enhancing properties. The flavor of the indigenous chocolate drink remained repellent to the Spanish palate—but not for long.

Due to the influence of indigenous wives and mistresses, as well as female servants, and their indigenous culinary practices, Spanish men developed a palate for the flavors of New Spain. In the early colonial days, chocolate, which had always been prepared by women in Mesoamerica, did not undergo a change in preparation. It was still sweetened with honey, with ground-up dried flowers such as *xochinacaztli* for a slightly bitter taste, or the peppery tasting *mecaxóchitl* small flowers, as well as *tlilxochitl* vanilla, and the achiote seeds that gave it its red color. Even after more Spanish women began to arrive in New Spain in the late 1520s, their Creole children—offspring of two Spanish parents, but born in the Americas—were suckled by Maya wet nurses and fed by indigenous women servants.[110] Dr. Marcy Norton, a historian of the early Atlantic world, argues that "the Spanish did not alter chocolate to fit the predilections of their palate. Instead, Europeans unwittingly developed a taste for Indian chocolate, and they sought to re-create the indigenous chocolate experience in America and in Europe."[111]

In a decree of 1503, the Spanish Crown initiated the institution that would control and administer all commercial law. *La Casa de Contratación de las Indias*—the House of Trade of the Indies—was located in Seville. It collected all colonial duties and taxes, controlled all trade and voyages, and licensed sea captains and their vessels. The precision of its record keeping remains an admirable feat. It is fascinating to find Catalina Bustamante on the passenger list in the records of *La Casa de Contratación de las Indias*. The list indicates that she departed from Sanlúcar de Barrameda, Spain on 5 May 1514 with her husband Pedro Tinoco, her two daughters María and Francisca and her sisters-in-law, Juana and María.[112]

Fourteen years later, Catalina was widowed. An educated woman, committed to the ideals of the Franciscan tertiary order, she volunteered to start the school, and to teach reading, arithmetic, and catechism to the noble indigenous girls in Texcoco. In addition, she wanted to acculturate the indigenous noble girls in her care to the Spanish ways. Thus, she taught them to speak Castilian Spanish and to run a household in the Spanish tradition. But the noble girls in her care had personal servants, girls of a low social rank, who kept the old indigenous traditions alive. The noble girls were served chocolate, befitting their high social rank, and supplied with gold jewels and shawls woven in the Aztec tradition, despite the laws forbidding this. The list of laws that condemned customs and practices from central Mexican Inquisitorial trials are long and harsh. Indigenous people were punished for disregarding Christian festivals, for practicing rain divination, making cacao offerings, and much more.[113]

In 1545 the collection of extensive laws pertaining to the Indies was printed in Mexico City. In addition to those laws, there were letters, ordinances, instructions, and provisions from the Crown to the governance of the Indies, much of it conflicting, but reflecting the fiscal control of all transatlantic goods. José Veitia Linaje, an official of *La Casa de Contratación*, circa 1620, wrote:

> Its jurisdiction is as large as its territory is boundless; its authority is so extraordinary that it has supplied the place of a Council, and has acted as such not only in reference to revenues and military affairs, with orders passing directly from the King to it; its wealth is such that none in Europe can compare with it; its credit so high that no private person could equal it.[114]

The merchant elite of Seville was composed of wealthy merchants, municipal leaders, clergy and nobility, and they had substantial influence and power. Initially, their early sixteenth-century trade bounty did not include large quantities of cacao. What the records indicate is that the amounts imported into Seville from the New World were for personal use. For example, a fifty-pound cargo of chocolate and the accompanying eight drinking vessels, known as *jícaras,* would be consumed by a household and guests over a few months.[115]

The Spanish men who permanently returned to Spain were known as *indianos,* a word indicating their long-residence in the Indies. In order to satisfy their new personal taste for chocolate, the *indianos* brought it back with them, along with Mesoamerican spices for the drink they had learned to enjoy. Clerics had also assimilated the habit of drinking chocolate in the New World, and transported chocolate back to Europe for their own use, and as small gifts or "bribes to facilitate whatsoever just or unjust, right or wrong, they are to demand."[116] In fact, it's been said that "chocolate lubricated social relations among different groups of elite Andualusia, Spain."[117]

With such far-reaching powers of control by the Crown and its institu-
tions, it is most likely that at first the export of cacao was a nominal amount for
personal use or as gift to a monastery or convent back in Spain. Contraband on
a larger scale could not have escaped the long arm of *La Casa de Contratación*.
Dr. Marcy Norton estimates that the majority of transatlantic passengers were
clergy and merchants who had grown accustomed to consuming chocolate in
the Americas and had introduced chocolate to Europe.[118]

The question of who served the first cup of chocolate in Spain remains
an enigma. Some authors and scholars seem to latch on to legends and turn
them into fact. In 1992 I was granted permission to research certain records
in the Archives of the Indies in Seville. At that time, I was focused on a genealogical search, but since there is a link between chocolate and my Basque ancestors, I cross-referenced dates and the main historical characters often cited
in studies of chocolate. Afterwards I researched geography, cultural traditions,
and the religious orders involved, and dissected facts within the legends of
chocolate. It is my conclusion that the actions of certain religious orders
were the impetus that transferred the chocolate-drinking tradition from New
Spain to Seville.

The key date is the 1544 voyage by Bartolomé de las Casas from Guatemala to Spain. His was the first voyage that documents cacao as cargo. Prior to
1544, neither Hernán de Cortés nor Christopher Columbus ever documented
any cacao shipments on board their voyages back to Spain. However, by 1544,
the Franciscan and Dominican Roman Catholic orders were well entrenched
in the religious life of New Spain, and their clerics had made return voyages
across the Atlantic. It is reasonable to assume that they carried small quantities
of cacao back to Spain.

Flemish friar Pedro de Gante and two fellow Franciscans accompanied
Hernán Cortés on his invasion of Mexico. Pedro de Gante is credited for creating
the first school for indigenous boys in New Spain—Colegio Santiago Tlatelolco,
founded in 1528, near the famous Mesoamerican market of Tlatelolco where
cacao was the currency and chocolate was served copiously. Pedro de Gante also
taught religion and art to Diego de Valadés, the first mestizo friar to be ordained
in New Spain. Valadés wrote and illustrated the *Rhetorica Christiana,* printed in
1579 in Perugia, Italy, which describes the evangelization and conversion of the
indigenous people of New Spain.[119]

Among the twenty-seven engravings in the book is "The Great Chain
of Being," a depiction of Christian cosmology. This hierarchy includes God
seated on a throne at the heavenly top, with lower levels of saints, souls, birds,
and trees. In the center of the tree level, a cacao tree is shielded by a taller,

FIG. 50

shade-giving tree. The fusion of the Mesoamerican belief in the sacredness of cacao within a Christian paradise is significant in that this image was created by an ordained Franciscan friar, who had the audacity to promote an amalgamation of his mother's indigenous beliefs and those of the European clerics who had ordained him. Additionally, it's been noted that "chocolate escaped the condemnation of the friars, as it fell under the label of benign, neutral, material culture."[120]

Later in the history of the colonial era, chocolate consumption lost its benign reputation and devolved into something more sinister, which drew the attention of the Inquisition. Nonetheless, the engraving of "The Great Chain of Being" demonstrates that indigenous converts to Christianity retained links to their ancient beliefs through the entire cycle of cacao to chocolate, and its beverage and foam rituals—despite the rigorous assimilation and acculturation dogma imposed by the Church and the Crown.[121]

There are several similarities between my convent school in Quito, Ecuador circa 1960 and the school started by Catalina Bustamante Tinoco in Mexico in 1528. Both were fortresses against the outside world. The inside world was ruled by strict disciplinarian teachers who took a brimstone-and-fire approach to faith. In the process, the joy of the Christian message was difficult for the students to find.

In the case of the school run by Catalina Bustamante Tinoco, the outside world crashed in on May 1529. Juan Peláez de Berrio, the Spanish mayor of the town of Antequera del Valle de Guaxaca, sent two indigenous henchmen to jump the walls of the convent school and rape a particular noble indigenous girl, with whom he was obsessed, and also rape her servant. Despite the involvement of Bishop Juan de Zumárraga's troops, Juan Peláez de Berrio avoided any severe punishment other than a fine for "moral damages suffered by the girls."[122] For several years, Catalina Bustamante Tinoco continued to pressure Bishop Zumárraga to punish the mayor and his henchmen. She even returned to Spain to plead with the monarchs.

Within a decade, the town of Texcoco, where the school was located, underwent social upheaval, resulting in the 1539 public burning at the stake of Don Carlos Ometochtli, the ruler of Texcoco. Bishop Zumárraga was determined to punish the indigenous leader for continuing ancient religious practices that the Church wished to destroy.[123] Catalina and her entire family perished during the pandemic known as the *cocoliztli* or great pestilence. Characterized by high fevers and bleeding, it killed 800,000 people in the Valley of Mexico between 1545 to 1547.[124]

The outside political world crashed into my convent school with the deadly coup d'état that frightened the Spanish nuns into scurrying back to their native land. For centuries, convent schools represented unrealistic wishes for a cloistered setting where young girls could be shielded from the harsh realities of life. They were also places where many families locked away the excess daughters, spinster aunts or lonely widows, cloistered against their wishes. Along with catechism, and the academic subjects of the times, the female students also learned to hold on to their traditions as a way of anchoring themselves to a culture that was fading away, as in the convent in Texcoco. In my case, I learned to cherish the small comforts—a cup of hot chocolate, the sweet memory of slurping fresh cacao pulp or an Andean fairy tale told to me by my nanny, which reminded me of home.

For most convent girls throughout time, the convent was not a home away from home. For the religious women who chose to live in convents, the cloistered life was indeed their home. The constants in the life of a convent are prayer, song, labor, and food or fast. The importance of chocolate as a traditional ritual persisted in the convents of New Spain, but chocolate also impacted the daily lives of the convents back in Spain, where the chocolate drink evolved into a money-making enterprise for creative nuns renowned for their culinary talents.

FIG. 51

Convents and Cultural Fusion

THE HERMETICALLY SEALED FRONT DOOR OF MY CHILDHOOD CONVENT WAS AS difficult to pry open as an airtight coffin. A knock on our convent door always sent waves of excitement among the nuns and the few boarding students. Our porter was the heftiest and most menacing of the nuns. With her every counterclockwise turn of the many door locks, the convent came alive with anticipation of a visitor from the outside world. Even if someone had charged in through the now-opened door, he or she would have only made it to an airless, small parlor. This is where a guest had to sit and wait for the lucky nun or student to enter through a back door. A dividing, carved-wood grille in the parlor separated the visitor from the cloistered girl.

Men, in particular, received the porter's most menacing welcome. Over the years that I lived there, the porter grew accustomed to the periodic presence of my bespectacled and bespoke-tailored father. A well-known prosecutor, he was severely courteous, and ignored her brusqueness. He thanked her for keeping an eye on me, and always handed her a box of chocolate candies. She quickly hid her undeserved reward in the folds of her thick white habit, salivating at the chocolaty treat to come, and escorted him to the parlor, known as a *locutorio*.

Once he sat down across from me, I tried to impress him by reciting the poems I had memorized on the chance he would visit. He tried, in vain, to hug me through the grille, to lift me up like he did when I was a kindergartner. In court he was known for his unrelenting drilling of a witness on the stand, but in the convent he was defeated by the grille, and by the hopelessness of divorce. On one visit, my father handed me two boxes of chocolates and a delicate doll with tanned skin and a Hawaiian straw skirt. I should have suspected something was awry when he gave me that extra box of chocolates, but instead, I attempted to hug him. The wood grille impeded his warm grasp of me. My father simply gave up and walked away—never to be seen again.

The women who entered the cloistered convents in Spain and Spanish America knew full well that they would remain shuttered there for the rest of their lives. Their entrance through the convent doors was their farewell to their families. Depending on the convent, the nuns were allowed sporadic visits from female family members only. However, certain brilliant and well-known nuns, and those with the highest social connections, were allowed to have high-ranking male visitors. The sixteenth-century Spanish Saint Theresa of Avila grew disillusioned after many male intellectual visitors, known as *devotos,* visited her parlor in the Carmelite convent. She received permission to found an austere order of Discalced Carmelites. The nuns from this same order in New Spain were known as the only nuns who were forbidden from drinking chocolate, and survived on bread and water.[125] In the San Jerónimo convent, Sor Juana Inés de la Cruz, the savant, noted poet and accountant, entertained visiting *vicereines*, bishops, and other dignitaries until past eleven in the evening, on many occasions—and she refused to give it up.

According to Dr. Asunción Lavrin, one of the first women to receive a doctorate from Harvard Graduate School of Arts and Science, many women in sixteenth-to-eighteenth century Spain and Spanish America renounced their families and homes to live in a cloistered convent because of their religious conviction, while many others succumbed to economic and familial circumstances and entered a convent reluctantly.[126] All of the women in a convent took a pledge of obedience and humility. However, the hierarchy of the convents reflected the world outside the convent walls. While wealthy nuns who entered the convent with large dowries lived in vast and luxurious cell-apartments, their servants and slaves lived in poverty. Dr. Lavrin's research on the convents of New Spain revealed that the nuns included chocolate in their budget since they consumed it daily. In fact, the nuns "kept the chocolate in small boxes in their cells."[127]

The difference in convent lifestyles was extreme between the wealthy nuns, with opulent lives, and their poor novice servants, known as *niñas* or girls, despite their advanced age.[128] The condition of the slaves was generally abject poverty. The ongoing concern for all members of the convents was the financial condition of their convent. In general, most convents lacked sufficient income from the dowries and endowments, and the nuns—or more likely, their servants—prepared items for sale in their communities. Ostensibly, the nuns kept busy because of Saint Jerome's admonition that an idle mind is the devil's workshop and idle hands his tools. In reality, it was the continuous need for funds which pushed the convents into commerce. The rhyming motto at the convents was: *Oran y Laboran*—They Pray and They Work.

FIG. 52

The 2017 exhibition from the John Carter Brown Library, *Women of the Page: Convent Culture in the Early Modern Spanish World*, depicted the lives of the nuns revolving around rituals of fasting and feasting.[129] Food was the center of celebration and hospitality and chocolate was a key element of the nuns' diet. In a letter written by a nun named María de José in the late seventeenth-century, she apologizes for the brown blotches on her manuscript: the boy serving the choco-late, she says, spilled it on her notebook. The exhibit shows that the convent nuns were recognized for the elaborate and costly meals they prepared for special guests. The cookbook displayed in this exhibit, *Arte de Cocina, Pasteleria, Vizcocheria, y Conserveria*, or The Art of Cooking, Pastry, Biscuits, and Confectionery, was written by Francisco Martínez Montiño and first published in 1611. It describes the extent of the sweet treats sold by convents across Spain and its colonies.[130]

Convents sold three main items: needlework, herbal medicine, and desserts along with chocolate. Some convents in Spain and in its colonies were known for their exquisite trousseau needlework, some others for their herbal tonics, but all of the convents in the Hispanic world specialized in sweet treats that brought them a continuous stream of income.

Each convent in a town tried to create unique and memorable treats to lure buyers, not only during the Catholic holidays when townspeople expected the nuns to outdo themselves, but throughout the year. Competition for the tastiest desserts among the convents was high, and this impelled the nuns to become very creative—and secretive—with their recipes.

The origin of the art of pastries, confectionery, syrups, and tonics was the Muslim culture that ruled the Iberian Peninsula from 711CE to 1492CE. In her book *L'Europe se Met á Table (Europe Sits at the Gastronomic Table)*, French culinary history expert Liliane Plouvier calls Spain *"la première terre confiturière d'Europe,"* the first confectionery country in Europe, due to its Al-Ándalus heritage.[131] (Al-Ándalus, the southernmost region of Spain, has been known as Andalusia since the reconquest of 1492.) Plouvier identifies this heritage as the source of many European desserts, as well as critical to pharmaceutical and gastronomical advances. She cites numerous sugar, herbs, and fruit lozenges that derived from Arab medicinal culture. Additionally, she contends that Spain was the first country to create syrups and tonics in Europe based on the *jarabe* syrup of the Arab world.[132]

FIG. 53

FIG. 55

The convents in the Spanish world concocted medicinal syrups that brought much-needed income to their convents, and health relief to the locals who bought their medicines. However, just as the dominant Spanish landowners wrested cacao cultivation and trade in the colonies away from indigenous women, the formation of apothecary guilds in Spain undermined the work of the convents. The guilds of *boticarios* required passing an exam after four years of practice, as well as a knowledge of Latin:[133] both requirements could have been met by many nuns in many convents. However, women were not allowed in the guilds, and medicinal products from convents were commercially diminished by those of the *boticarios.*

Liliane Plouvier credits the Andalusians with pioneering the culinary use of puff pastry, donuts, sugar, sorbet, jam, candies, candied fruit, marmalades, marzipan and nougat, rose water, orange blossom water, and sweet and sour flavors.[134] The specific Andalusian desserts that started the dough ball rolling are described in the culinary history book *La cocina hispano-magrebí durante la época almohade (The Hispanic-Maghreb Cookbook During the Almohad Era)* by Ambrosio Huici Miranda. A description of one of the ancient Arab desserts took my breath away. He describes a pastry I remember from my childhood, but its origin was in 711CE. It is called *almojábanas*—dough stuffed with cheese, deep fried, and sprinkled with powdered sugar.[135] Ambrosio Huici Miranda notes that Arab desserts introduced cane sugar to Spain, as the Arabs had access to processed sugar cane from the ninth century. Ivan Day, an expert in historic food, writes that "sugar was by far the most important material" in developing the art of confectionery.[136]

Huici Miranda describes *cuernos de gacela* or Gazelle's Horns, a tea cookie made with sugar, ground almonds, grated lemon, and egg. Their curved horn shape does, in fact, look like the brown ears of the Curier's gazelles I've seen when hiking the stony Atlas Mountains of Morocco. During the Muslim reign in Spain, there was a long period of time dubbed *La Convivencia*, an era when people of the three religions in Al-Ándalus—Islam, Judaism, and Christianity—lived in harmony. This ended with the Edict of Expulsion of 1492, leaving Jews and Muslims with an ungodly choice: convert to Catholicism, leave the country, or die. So when I read Ambrosio Huici Miranda's description of the Sephardic Jewish dessert dating back to the time of *La Convivencia*, I choked up. Every Christmas, my late mother spent several days making a type of beignet or fritter covered in a spiced honey syrup. In Ecuador we called this beignet a *pristiño,* and it is the same as the Sephardic Jewish buñuelo. In Al-Ándalus, this was served during *Jáneca* (Hanukah). Sadly, since my mother's passing no one in the family can bear to prepare it. For me, its fragrant syrup remains loaded with memories of affliction and with the calamity that my Sephardic ancestors had to endure.

The convent nuns also sold *buñuelos* with their own delectable syrup. They took advantage of the fusion of cultures, drawing on their storied history as remarkable pastry chefs, confectioneries, nougat creators, and molasses mavens to create more and more unique desserts. They utilized the fruits from their orchards, along with cinnamon, cloves, and saffron, to make jams and marmalades, and an array of mouthwatering *bocadillos,* or bite-size treats. Nuns hoarded the secrets of making chocolate in the fragrant and spicy way of Mesoamerica. However, through the decades, they slowly modified the chocolate from being served cold to serving it thick and hot. Due to limited access to the fragrant flowers from the colonies, they added cinnamon and replaced the honey with more sugar. Marcy Norton suggests that when "Spaniards tinkered with the recipes by using Old World spices, they were actually trying to stimulate the flavors offered by less available New World flowers."[137] They employed a wooden *molinillo* or stirring stick to make the required foam, but its spiritual symbolism from Mesoamerica was obliterated.

Each of the convents in Seville, and those throughout Spanish America, had its own sweet specialties for sale. To make the sale, convents used a small lazy Susan, known as a *torno,* accessed through a tiny door in the convent walls. This would enable the exchange of money for treat without face-to-face contact. At the convents in Seville, the nun attending the *torno* would say: "Hail Mary full

*¡El dinero habla,
el chocolate canta!*
Money talks,
chocolate sings!

of Grace," to which the customer would respond, "Conceived without sin." The *tornos* are still used in some cloistered convents in Seville.[138]

Numerous sweets that the nuns originated are sold to this day. At the convent of San Leandro, it's been possible to buy their famous *yemas* since the sixteenth century. The recipe remains a secret, but its ingredients are eggs, sugar, and lemon. The convent of Santa María de Jesús is responsible for introducing the precursor to the *churro* fritter, known worldwide. In its original form it was known as a *rosco frito*, and the nuns dipped it into their hot chocolate drink. This convent is credited with making the first chocolate cake, centuries ago, and the torrone, the nougat confection inspired by a Muslim-era dessert, a small square made from honey, egg whites, and toasted almonds. The convent of San Clemente specialized in marzipan and marmalade delicacies that featured the fruit from their orchards, and the convent of Santa Paula also drew from their extensive orchard of figs and other fruit trees in numerous dessert recipes. Some confections were given comical and disrespectful names by the outside community, like the bishop's tongue or the nuns' pinches.

In Seville, nuns acknowledge the ancient Al-Ándalus heritage of sugar as confectionery. To this day, they offer snacks for sale called *bocadillos árabes,* bite-size Arab treats. The nuns developed the art of confectionery by adding citrus, spices, almond, pistachio, rosewater, and chocolate. Based on their success with marzipan shaped fruits and flowers, their knowledge of thickening agents increased. Therefore, the convent nuns must be given credit for creating the first chocolate bite-size treat and the first chocolate cake.

However, the guild of confectioneries, allied with the powerful commercial entities of Spain, constrained the ingenuity of the nuns. To add insult to injury, subsequent cultures have claimed to be the first to introduce chocolate confections in Europe, without even giving a nod to the resourceful and imaginative nuns of the Spanish Empire who were the true pioneers of chocolate confections in Europe.

Revenge with Chocolate

*D*ESPITE THE CULINARY INNOVATIONS IN THE CONVENT KITCHENS OF THE SPANISH world, the far-reaching ecclesiastic authorities sought to root out any scent of chocolate malfeasance. As more and more chocolate from the colonies arrived in Spain, the church began to examine its consumption with the tenacity of a sniffing dog seeking a buried bone. Their olfactory suspicions increased with each cross-Atlantic voyage, and the church grew determined to punish chocolate impropriety in its realms.

Doctor Martha Few, author of *Chocolate, Sex, and Disorderly Women in Late-Seventeenth and Early-Eighteenth Century Guatemala,* asserts that chocolate was a "central vehicle of women's ritual power, used as the basis for magical potions to cast supernatural illness, in sexual witchcraft practices, and even, at times, as a flash point for women's disorderly behavior in public settings."[139] The initial bone of contention about chocolate was an unresolved matter debated by Catholic theologians for over a century: whether drinking chocolate broke the mandated church fasts. If it was determined that chocolate was a food, then its consumption would break the fast, but if it was ruled as a drink, then it would be permitted. In 1662, Pope Alexander VII ruled that chocolate did not violate the fasts and could be consumed during the imposed church fast days, such as Fridays and during Lent.

By the time of his decision, the demographics of the colonies had changed dramatically. The Church, part of the elite class, realized that the population had become a mix of European, mestizo, indigenous, and African, and their fusion of beliefs "proved a fertile ground for the flowering of a popular magical and religious cultures beyond their control."[140] Children born—often out of wedlock—to indigenous women and Spanish fathers were known as mestizos and ranked as *gente de razón*, or people of reason. They faced the full force of the church authorities. In a climate of social flux and injustice, women resorted to magical acts to attract a specific man, maintain a man's love interest, or to reject him; it could also be used against abusive husbands.[141] The use of chocolate in such "disorderly behavior," as Dr. Few asserts, transformed chocolate into an ingredient seen as potentially dangerous.[142]

FIG. 55

The most extreme use of sorcery with chocolate was reserved for deadly retaliation against a man. Ruth Behar's research into the inquisitorial records of colonial Mexico reveals numerous instances of women using food or drink—and concocting what they believed were magical potions—to help them achieve their goals. Behar writes of a woman who was afraid that her husband might stray during a trip away from her: following the directions of a female sorcerer, she mixed her "menstrual blood and hairs from shameful parts" in a cup of chocolate and made her husband drink it.[143]

The desire to tame men and to stop their physical abuse drove women to adding poisonous substances to the chocolate they served them. Women could use doctored chocolate to control men's sexual behavior or retaliate against their husbands' aggression.[144] In the essay "Chocolate and Sinful Behaviors: Inquisition Testimonies," the authors explain the reasons why chocolate was used as a vehicle of witchcraft. Chocolate was thick and its dark properties would mask many pulverized substances. Its generally bitter taste would mask "ill-flavors that resulted from the addition of crow's heart, excrement, human flesh, and menstrual blood."[145] There are several cases on record where women, charged by the Inquisition, admitted to using a range of potions and harmful agents in cups of chocolate. On April 7, 1621, Juan Martinez-Commissioner of the Holy Office of the Inquisition in Guadalajara, New Spain, noted that Doña Juana de Bracamonte had been given worms, called *esticulinos,* by an Indian woman. She was led to believe that if she put the worms in her husband's chocolate his abuse would stop, and she would tame him.[146]

Elite Spanish women also resorted to consulting female sorcerers for witchcraft using chocolate. According to Dr. Few's archival research in Santiago de Guatemala, a wealthy Spanish woman named Doña Luisa de Gálvez paid a woman to act as intermediary with an indigenous sorcerer named María de Zumagra, who could supply three packets of powders needed for sexual witchcraft. The intermediary was a mestizo woman, Gerónima de Varaona, who instructed Doña de Gálvez on the use of the powders. She was to wash her private parts with water and use that water for the chocolate drink for the male victim, and then she was to mix the powders into the chocolate. De Varaona's statement reveals that she helped Doña de Gálvez because she feared the violent reputation of the Spanish woman: Doña de Gálvez was known as "La Machete" because she could "cut out the tongue with a machete."[147]

Dr. Few cites another example of Spanish women using indigenous sorcerers, knowledgeable in the use of chocolate with the addition of various powders, to retaliate against abusive husbands. A Spanish seamstress, María de los Ángeles, also washed her genitals with the same water employed to make chocolate. She added black powers into the customary *jícara,* a gourd cup, and served the drink to her abusive husband in order to "free him from his anger."[148] Using the same witchcraft of magical powders stirred into chocolate, another

Spanish woman asked an indigenous sorcerer, named Anita, to free her male partner from his anger.[149]

Instances of chocolate sorcery were numerous throughout the colonies. Men began to fear drinking a cup of chocolate given to them by women who might seek to retaliate against them or to make them impotent.[150] Women might be the recipients of a poisoned cup of chocolate from a female competitor. Dr. Few's research in the Inquisitional archives reveals a case of a notorious woman María de Santa Inés, known as "*La Panecito*" or the small bread, who would give poisoned chocolate bread to her enemies.

Women often freely confessed their chocolate malfeasance to the Inquisition, either because of their fear of punishment for not confessing or because of psychological pressure. The authors of *Chocolate: History, Culture, and Heritage* conclude that unlike crimes like heresy, for which punishment was burning at the stake, chocolate crimes committed by women were seen by the Inquisition tribunals as minor.[151] The Inquisition often treated the women's offenses with leniency. However, when the tribunal decided on relaxation—that is, execution—they turned over the condemned heretic to the secular authorities.

The inquisitors in Spain were also lenient with cases of witchcraft since they felt the women acted out of ignorance. They believed that the accused witches were unfortunate women who should be pitied and not blamed. In 1554, the grand inquisitor Fernando de Valdés stated that women accused of witchcraft could be made to confess anything.[152] In Valencia, Spain, witches were charged for "procuring beverages designed to favor illegitimate love affairs or cure the sick."[153] The beverages were not identified, but since the trade of cacao was in full force, and Valencia is a port city, receiving cargo from various ports in the realm, it is likely that the beverage was chocolate—a thick, dark, foreign-tasting drink that could easily be doctored with poisons.

Throughout the Spanish realm, the punishment for witchcraft varied, but generally, the most common sanctions for witches were: banishment to a different locale; fines; public whippings; and being paraded, naked to the waist and riding on mules, while villagers pelted them with onions.[154] It wasn't until November 1610, and the notorious witch trials of Zugarramurdi in the Guipuzcoa region of the Basque country of Spain, that eleven witches were burned in effigy and six died in the flames in an infamous auto-da-fé.

These witch trials and the corresponding myths about my Basque ancestors have persisted in my family lore. Our ancestral village of Velástegui is only 45 miles away from the village of Zugarramurdi, where the accused witches lived. To this day, the dominant language in Guipuzcoa is Basque, an enigma of a language that has no Indo-European foundation, has been spoken in situ for thousands of years back to prehistory—and is a real tongue-twister that has defeated me. Many small towns in the Basque country remain secluded due to decades of living under the oppression of the Franco regime (1935-1975) and also affected by the Basque separatist organization, Basque Homeland and Liberty, known as ETA and active from 1959. (ETA's armed activity ceased in 2011.)

The relevance of the 1610 auto-da-fé during Spain's colonial expansion is the fact that the Basque women accused of witchcraft were the wives, sisters, mothers, daughters of Basque merchant sailors who were away in the Indies. On Christopher Columbus first voyage, not only were the shipmasters Basques, but the ships were built in Basque shipyards. My own ancestor Ojer de Velástegui was the scribe aboard the *Pinta,* and many of the crew were Basques. Known for their

FIG. 56

close-knit communities and maritime expertise, these mariners acted collectively, although among each other they could be very competitive.

The Basques were also adroit at transporting contraband. It is highly probable that they brought cacao back to the Basque country in the sixteenth and seventeenth-centuries, which led to the later prominence of chocolate commerce in the Basque country. Its proximity to the French border, and to their Basque brethren in the Pays Basque of southern France, led to the introduction of chocolate, adopted by the French elite class and popular in the salons of French nobility.

The Basque women who stayed behind kept the agrarian economy—sheep herding and the wool trade—alive in the Basque hinterlands while their men were away in the colonies. It's been speculated through the centuries that the Basque women's hard work, often well into the night, made neighbors suspicious of their activities and envious of their dedication. They turned them into the Inquisition, alleging their participation in witches' covens sprinkled throughout the foggy hills and hidden valleys of Guipuzcoa.

My ghoulish interest in and repulsion for the instruments of torture started at as a preteen when I visited a torture dungeon tourist attraction in San Francisco. As I walked from the infamous rack, where the hands and feet of the accused were chained to a roller that the torturer turned until joints were dislocated, to the *strappado* where the accused was left hanging by the arms until he or she confessed, I realized that my Spanish ancestors had been the creators of most these abhorrent instruments of torture. I couldn't fathom anyone inflicting such pain on another person in order to extract confessions of alleged crimes against the Catholic church. I realized that undergoing this type of severe torture would make anyone admit to anything just to make the pain stop. Years later, when I read about British women branded on the face as punishment for their petty theft of chocolate, centuries after the 1610 auto-da-fé in the Basque country, I understood the meaning of history repeating itself.

Chocolate Crime and Punishment

The fictional character of Moll Flanders kept popping into my mind when I read about the British women sentenced at the Old Bailey for chocolate-related crimes in Louis Grivetti's essay *Chocolate, Crime, and the Courts: Selected English Trial Documents, 1693-1834*. Daniel Defoe's 1722 picaresque novel *Moll Flanders* recounts the fortunes and misfortunes of a poor woman, a felon transported to Virginia. Moll's life was a series of misadventures, which she managed to survive due to her moxie and resilience.

Grivetti's research on the British court documents reveals that thirty percent of the accused chocolate thieves at the Old Bailey were poor women who had previous offences, and their preferred method of larceny was by breaking and entering homes or businesses.[155] Most of the chocolate-associated crimes were crimes of opportunity or spur-of-the-moment decisions.[156] During the era researched, chocolate was a rare and expensive commodity, similar in economic value to gold or silver.[157] So it's unsurprising that cacao beans, ground cacao, manufactured chocolate, and chocolate serving equipment and utensils were stolen.

I suspect many of impoverished women thieves had backgrounds like Moll's. She encounters many unbelievable and unimaginable circumstances, but survives her trials and tribulations and lives to age seventy. Along her long journey, Moll lives by her wits; she is a carefree and immoral character, but still sympathetic.

Among the long list of female felons uncovered in the archives of the Old Bailey by Grivetti, I had hoped to read a few acquittals of the chocolate thieves. Instead, there were numerous women sentenced to be transported to Australia or the American colonies. On September 9, 1772, Elizabeth Wood (alias Smith) was found guilty of chocolate grand larceny and sentenced to be transported.

FIG. 57

The duration and location were not listed. On April 9, 1823, Catherine Riley was found guilt of receiving stolen goods and transported for 14 years. Letitia Padwick, guilty of chocolate grand larceny, was also transported for 14 years.

The other punishments were whipping and branding. On April 24, 1745 Jane Rankin was branded for simple grand larceny of chocolate. According to the Old Bailey records, branding took place in the courtroom, immediately after sentencing. The brand was placed on the thumb or on the cheek. On May 26, 1784, Christina Wigmore was privately whipped and sentenced to hard labor for six months in the House of Corrections for the same simple grand larceny of chocolate.

The fictional character of Moll Flanders lives in dire poverty until the night she finds an unguarded package and steals it. After her initial sense of remorse, she finds that she has a talent for theft and soon accumulates stolen goods. In the novel Defoe depicts the bottom rung of society, especially the destitute, lonely women who were forced to survive at any cost. However, in the essay "Convict Transportation and Penitence in *Moll Flanders*," Gabriel Cervantes contends that to some historians, the novel can be read as propaganda in favor of the British American system of transporting indentured servants to its colonies.[158] This system used indentured servants as a means of expanding the British market for exports, without labor costs.

The reality for the women sentenced by being transported to the colonies was harsh and bleak. The societal view of incarcerated women was that the women were prostitutes, unmarriageable reprobates, or a corruptive force in the community.[159] In fact, prostitutes were not transported, and most of the women who were transported were convicted for thievery, and sentenced to seven years of indentured servitude in the British American colonies.

Other instances of chocolate infractions committed by women fall into their own outlier categories. The *New York Tribune* of January 31, 1885 reported a case involving a German woman, Emilie Sichel, who arrived in New York aboard the steamer *Egypt*. Her trunk was detained by custom inspector Robertson. He found ten pounds of chocolate, ten corsets, and some lace curtains. He declared the goods dutiable and placed the trunk in the public storehouse at the Inman Line Pier until Sichel paid the duty. A fire destroyed the pier and her trunk. Emilie Sichel sued the custom officers and as a result recovered four hundred and fifty-nine dollars.

Among the most celebrated chocolate crimes, there is one that borders on legend. It is the 1803 case of Napoleon Bonaparte's ex-lover and fellow Corsican, Pauline Riotti. After being jilted by Napoleon, Riotti found employment in the kitchen of Lyon Cathedral, where Bonaparte's half-uncle was archbishop. Knowing that Napoleon would be staying there for two days on his way to Italy, she offered to make his habitual cup of chocolate. Usually, Napoleon welcomed any affectionate attention from young women. However, in 1802 a woman named Charlotte Encore had thrown herself at his feet and then tried to embrace Napoleon. His grenadier guards spotted a stiletto hidden in her sleeve, and it was

56. NAPOLÉON Ier (1804-1815). *Le matin d'Austerlitz* (1805).

FIG. 58

determined that she was part of a larger plot to assassinate him. When Pauline Riotti served him the chocolate, the grenadier forced her to drink it before Napoleon took a sip. Within a short time, Pauline was dead.[160]

The legend of poisoned chocolate progressed through other European cities, with each new case of poison revealing tawdry facts worthy of fiction. There are credible facts in each of the incidents, but in most of the reported instances of poisoned chocolate, there is more lore, and an abundance of cautionary tales. One is a warning of the danger in May–December marriages. In 1667, a young beauty names Margaret Brooke married Sir John Denham, who was thirty years her senior. She had a very public affair with the Duke of York, the future King James II. His wife, the Duchess of York, detested Margaret and it's alleged that she supplied the poisoned chocolate that killed her young rival.

The *London Morning Post* of Friday, August 25, 1871 covered the sensational trial of Christina Edmunds in Brighton, a popular seaside town England. Edmunds had been rejected by her lover, one Dr. Beard, and decided to poison his wife. Anonymously she sent boxes of poisoned chocolate treats to several people, including Mrs. Beard, hoping she would not be discovered as the villainess. After the death of a four-year-old boy who had eaten her chocolate gift, police apprehended her. Edmunds was composed during her trial, never showing any remorse. She was sentenced to the Broadmoor criminal lunatic asylum where she lived until her death in 1903.

What was not deranged, but rather a screwball crime, was the antics of the high-class women of San Cristobal de las Casas, Mexico in 1625. Despite the repeated admonition of Bishop Bernardino de Salazar y Frías for the women to cease their chocolate consumption during Mass, the women were so accustomed to having their servants supply them with hot chocolate and treats at the cathedral, that they simply refused his command. These pampered women claimed to need stamina from drinking cups of chocolate in order to listen to the long sermon. They also claimed that without their chocolate their devotion would certainly weaken. The bishop would not allow the servants to serve chocolate: he refused their entry to the cathedral. When the women attended other churches instead, the bishop fumed and threatened excommunication. One day, he was served poison-laced chocolate—and died.

After his funeral, the unrepentant women returned to mass at the cathedral and enjoyed their cups of chocolate during Mass. It is said that after their defiant and vicious act against the bishop, the chocolate-loving townspeople said *"¡Le dieron su chocolate!"* This harsh retort means, "He got his just desserts."

FIG. 59

Chocolate and the European Aristocracy

ALTHOUGH BASQUE WOMEN WERE BURNED AT THE STAKE FOR THEIR ALLEGED witchcraft in Zugarramurdi, and female chocolate thieves in England were sentenced to 14 years of hard labor in the penal colonies, the noblewomen of France were undeterred. They grew enamored of chocolate to an unbelievable extent. They consumed it, wrote about it, turned it into a social event, and breathlessly proclaimed its qualities as an aphrodisiac. Their chocolate mania also led to advances in the chocolate culinary arts. The French aristocrats learned of chocolate's Mesoamerican reputation as a beverage exclusively for royalty, and they adopted it as a privilege of their elevated social class. According to food historian, Maricel E. Presilla, chocolate "arrived in Europe with the aura of an exotic luxury for the cognoscenti."[161]

The two Spanish princesses credited with bringing the ritual of drinking chocolate to France were Anne of Austria and María Teresa, both *Infantas,* a title given to the children of the king of Spain. In 1615, when they were both fourteen years old, Anne of Austria married King Louis XIII by proxy. When they were finally living together in France, neither one was attracted to the other, and Anne—who grew up in Madrid—found comfort in her Spanish ways. One of these habits was drinking chocolate and the other was eating garlicky food. Despite an often distant relationship with her husband, Anne gave birth to the future Louis XIV and Philippe, Duke of Orleans, when she was in her late 30s. However, the king never trusted her because of her allegiance to Spain and its interests.[162]

After her husband's death, Anne ensured that her oldest son—now King Louis XIV of France—married her niece, María Teresa of Spain. At their betrothal, María Teresa gave Louis a decorated chest full of chocolate as an engagement gift. During their marriage, she was devoted to the Sun King—and to drinking chocolate.

The wedding of 1660 was a political marriage to forge alliances between two powerful kingdoms. On November 7, 1659, both countries signed the Treaty of the Pyrenees. Shortly thereafter, Cardinal Mazarin told Queen Anne: "I bring your Majesty peace and the *Infanta.*"[163] The royal wedding took place on June 9, 1660 at the church of Saint Jean Baptiste in St. Jean-de-Luz, a border city between France and Spain, located on a natural harbor in the Bay of Biscay. In the seventeenth century, the British pirates called it the Viper's Nest since it was the secluded port of the Basque corsairs. These Basque sailors were famous for their whaling ventures to Newfoundland as early as 1500, for their cod fishing, and for their pirating. Since they also played a significant role as mariners to and from the Indies, they ignored the Crown and brought contraband chocolate to the Basque country from the early sixteenth century.

In 1992, when the waft of melting chocolate lured me into a small chocolate shop in Tolosa, Spain, I was more than surprised. I was blessed with travel serendipity—once again. The owner was a Basque man who had been trying to find the link to his ancestor who had sailed to Mexico around 1548, and never returned.

The chocolatier welcomed my first-person account of all things Aztec, especially my observations of the archeological sites of Central America. The shop owner's ancestors, former whalers and candlemakers (using whale spermaceti wax), had become chocolatiers centuries earlier after receiving cacao beans from Mexico through their Basque sailing connections. In his museum around the corner from his chocolate shop, he explained how the process of melting wax into molds for candles led to the melting of chocolate, which—when combined with the expertise of confectionary—resulted in exquisite chocolate treats. His museum provided a wealth of chocolate information through its exhibit of ancient tools of the trade, and was a trendsetter in private museum collections. He was also instrumental in providing me with books, printed in the Basque country, which proved that my ancestor Ojer de Velástegui had participated as a scribe on the *Pinta* of Christopher Columbus fame.

Once I understood the chocolate connection between the Basque chocolatiers of the sixteenth and seventeenth century and the Sephardic Jews expelled from Spain and Portugal, but welcomed to settle in the French Basque city of Bayonne in 1550, I was able to connect the dots between the ample availability of chocolate in France at the time of the wedding of Louis XIV of France and María Teresa of Spain in St. Jean-de-Luz, a mere 15 miles south of Bayonne. The Spanish crown sought an iron grip on the cultivation, distribution, and sale of cacao and chocolate, but both were escaping through its borders as easily as sand trickling from a fist.

FIG. 60

In 2018, I visited St. Jean-de-Luz once again. The tall and imposing altarpiece of the church of Saint Jean Baptiste is covered in gold from the Americas, and a large wooden Basque boat hangs opposite the entrance. The boat is a tribute to the daring Basque sailing expeditions to the New World. This church is unique for its three tiers of galleries on both sides of the church, a reminder

FIG. 61

that once this church was packed with dignitaries attending the wedding of two powerful royal families.

Today, the pedestrian old-town of St. Jean-de-Luz has many chocolate shops. The elegant timber houses, painted bright red and white, display immense clusters of red-hot chili peppers, originally brought from Mexico. The vacationers in this vibrant beach resort stroll in the sun unaware of the riches of the Americas that still glow in this former pirate lair. Lamentably, I found out that by 1725 the Bayonne Jewish chocolatiers were prohibited from making or selling chocolate. Some of them moved to Nantes, France, but most sailed to Curaçao and other islands in Caribbean, where they joined fellow Sephardic Jews who were already participating in cacao plantations and chocolate distribution.

After her marriage to the Sun King in 1660, the queen's name was modified to its French equivalent, Marie-Thérèse, but this did not help her to learn any French. She was adamant about speaking only Castilian Spanish and surrounded herself with Spanish ladies-in-waiting.[164] La Molina and La Philippa prepared the chocolate for the queen in the Spanish style. The Marquise de Montespan, a mistress of Louis XIV, wrote in her memoirs that:

> The Señora Molina, well furnished with silver kitchen utensils, has a sort of private kitchen or scullery reserved for her own use, and there it is that the manufacture takes place of clove scented chocolate, brown soups and gravies, stews redolent with garlic, capsicum, and nutmeg, and all that nauseous pastry which the young Infanta revels.[165]

Not only did Marie-Thérèse not speak French, she dressed frumpily compared with the extravagance of Versailles; she was not witty, and she could not amuse Louis XIV.[166] But she did produce an heir by 1661, and more children followed. Nonetheless, mean women at court, like the Duchesse d'Orléans, wrote that the queen had the constant habit of taking chocolate and that her teeth were broken, black, and ugly.[167] The Sun King approved of his cousin-wife—and of chocolate. Ultimately, he ordered it to be served three days a week in Versailles, where the women of the court learned to love it. He gave a royal patent for the manufacture and sale of chocolate to the protégé of his former mistress Olympe Mancini, a mean-spirited woman whose dimples and allure captivated the Sun King, but known as dubious, bold, and immoral.[168] Prior to the Sun King's wedding, Mancini—the niece of Cardinal Mazarin—constantly spoke ill of Marie-Thérèse.[169]

The refined women at the court of Louis XIV were valued for their ideas that flowed during conversation; they were cultured, brilliant, and elegant. Molière described them as the precious ones, *précieuses*.[170] From the correspondence of these women, we know a great deal about life in the court of Louis XIV. Among the most prolific and witty of these aristocrats was Madame de Sévigné, who wrote over one thousand descriptive and detailed letters, many addressed to her daughter, Madame de Grignan, who lived in Provence. In a letter dated February 11, 1671, she advises her daughter to drink chocolate to make her feel well again, and bemoans the fact that there are no chocolatiers near her daughter's estate. But later that year, on May 13, she admonishes her daughter for eating too much chocolate. Chocolate, she insists, is cursed, the cause of vapors and palpitations.[171]

In fact, Madame de Sévigné attributes her own colic and kidney infection to having consumed too much chocolate. In a letter of October 25, 1671, she worries that the chocolate her daughter is eating will burn her blood, and that rather than have miraculous effects, chocolate may hide something dark.[172] From Madame de Sévigné's correspondence, it is apparent that drinking chocolate had become a trend among French aristocrats, who discussed the benefits and possible health dangers from the medicine perspective of their time. Madame de Sévigné's name would continue into the twentieth-century when Auguste and Clementine Rouzaud launched the Marquise de Sévigné brand of chocolates in Vichy.[173]

The benefits of chocolate was a popular topic in letters shared among the witty ladies of the Sun King's court. In 1680, Marie de Villars, wife of the French ambassador to Spain, said she disliked most things Spanish with just one exception—chocolate, to which she attributed her good health.[174] Madame D'Aulnoy, a writer of fables, described attending a royal event where she was served chocolate in a new style of cup and saucer called a *mancerina*. This cup was named for its designer, the Marques de Mancera of Lima, Peru. It soon became the preferred chocolate drinking accessory in the royal courts of Europe

FIG. 63

since it prevented any chocolate spillage. The ingenious two-part design meant the handle-less chocolate cup fit into a saucer with a high ring in the middle, holding the cup in place. Although Madame D'Aulnoy praised the porcelain cup and the agate saucer trimmed with gold accents, she couldn't resist a jab about the addition of pepper and spices to the Spanish chocolate: using the same reasoning as Madame de Sévigné, she was astonished that the Spanish did not suffer internal burns.[175]

Following his field research in Mexico—and its findings, published in 1601—Spanish doctor Francisco Hernández promoted chocolate as an aphrodisiac. Dr. Hernández asserted that chocolate excited the venereal appetite, and the French aristocracy accepted this attribute as fact. This news excited the royal courts of Europe, and the legend of chocolate as an amorous drug persisted. By the reign of Louis XV, an avid chocolate drinker like his royal mistresses, chocolate's reputation as a sensual and erotic drink gained fame. Madame de Pompadour, his mistress for almost twenty years, beginning in 1745, was said to be a cold fish (her surname was Poisson, French for fish). It was assumed that she needed the sensual fortification of chocolate. She was also rumored to suffer from the sexually transmitted disease leukorrhea, and chocolate was believed to reduce the discharge. Madame du Barry, Louis XV's mistress from 1769 until his death in 1774, was another victim of slander. Her copious consumption of chocolate was said to make her extremely amorous. Both royal mistresses were rumored to have used chocolate to excite their lovers.[176] In 1785, the Marquis de Sade wrote about the erotic pleasures after imbibing chocolate in a harem, and its reputation as an aphrodisiac increased from the royal courts to the salons of Europe.

During Marie Antoinette's reign as Queen Consort (1774–1792), her requisite hot chocolate every morning at breakfast was copied by her hangers-on. Among her retinue was a Chocolate Maker to the Queen, who also used chocolate to make savory dishes very similar to the *mole* dishes of Oaxaca, Mexico, along with candies and biscuits, almost certainly based on the desserts made in convents. The French Revolution of 1789–1799—and its preferred form of punishment, the guillotine—ended the lives of Madame du Barry and Marie Antoinette, and the consumption of chocolate was reduced until the end of the Napoleonic wars. By 1815, the number of restaurants increased in France, and in Paris chocolate-making machines with steam engines began revolutionizing the industry, making chocolate products accessible to more people.[177]

Cioccolato in the Cinquecento
Chocolate in the 1500s in Italy

THE INTRODUCTION OF CHOCOLATE TO THE RENAISSANCE NOBILITY OF ITALY IS due, in part, to the influence of Spanish noblewomen who married into Italian aristocracy. These were strategic marriages, so Italians could benefit from the wealth and political support of the then-ruling Spanish empire. Up until the unification of the Kingdom of Italy in 1870, Italy as a nation did not exist. Naples, Sicily, Sardinia and Milan were under direct Spanish rule from 1409 to 1700, referred to as the Italian Indies.[178] Spanish viceroys in Naples, Palermo, and Cagliari—and the governor in Milan—all administered their regions in an unforgiving manner that promoted Spanish rule. The highborn Spanish brides marrying into old Italian families stubbornly and arrogantly maintained their cultural traditions—and drinking chocolate was de rigueur.

Throughout Spain's long dominance of the Kingdom of Naples and the Crown of Aragon in Sicily, nuns in the numerous cloistered convents developed Sicily's renowned pastry culture. It was also in these convents that Mexican-style chocolate tablets were made: they became the famous *Cioccolato di Modica*, the grainy-style chocolate bars of Modica in Sicily. *Cioccolato di Modica* is produced by manual grinding and uses a cold method whereby the chocolate paste and sugar are ground, and the cacao butter remains in the chocolate. The white patina is the result of the cacao butter blooming. It was usually flavored with cinnamon or vanilla, but today many other flavors are added. It can be eaten as a bar or dissolved in hot water as a beverage. This method of creating a chocolate tablet or bar to dissolve in hot water originated in the convents of New Spain—Mexico, during its colonial period.

UNESCO has recognized Modica for its baroque architecture, and it is also known as the town with one hundred churches, most of them rebuilt after the devastating earthquake of 1693. Modica was ruled by Spanish Admiral and Count of Modica, Federico Enriquez de Cabrera, and his powerful wife, Doña Ana de Cabrera y Moncada[179]—and then their descendants—from 1480 until 1700. The ruling admirals and counts of Modica, moving to Sicily from Spain, would have had access to cacao through Spanish maritime trade connections, and it's likely they drank chocolate, prepared by the nuns of Modica, as soon as it was first imported.

The connection of *cioccolato* to the Kingdom of Naples begins with Pedro Álvarez de Toledo, the Spanish Viceroy of Naples from 1532 to 1553. His exacting demands created the lasting architectural beauty of Naples, but his draconian insistence on the execution of petty thieves and obsession with the Inquisition made him a leader to fear. Only the powerful influence of the Sephardic Jewish financier Samuel Abravanel prevented the initiation of the Spanish Inquisition in Naples. The Spanish cultural influence in the Kingdom of Naples continued for centuries, and to this day the oldest quarters are known *Quartieri Spagnoli,* the Spanish quarters; the oldest churches have names like *San Giacomo degli Spagnoli* and *Santissima Trinità degli Spagnoli.*

In 1539, at the age of seventeen, the Viceroy's daughter, Leonor de Toledo (1522-1562), married Cosimo I de' Medici, Duke of Florence, in a spectacular wedding. Although Leonor had lived in Naples since the age of ten—and her

FIG. 64

name was modified to the Italian Eleonora di Toledo—she maintained her Spanish ways and tastes. She became a strong supporter of the Society of Jesus, an order founded in 1534 by Ignacio de Loyola, a Spanish Basque soldier turned priest. The Jesuits would soon dominate aspects of the cacao trade from the colonies. In 1773, for political reasons, they were suppressed and removed from Western Europe and its colonies by The Holy See. When the Jesuits finally left Mexico and arrived in the port of Cádiz, Spain in 1792, custom officials confiscated eight extremely heavy boxes of chocolate. Once opened at customs, the agents discovered smuggled, solid round gold bullion, covered in one-inch-thick chocolate.[180]

Cosimo I and Eleanora's descendant, Cosimo III de' Medici, Grand Duke of Tuscany (1642-1723), ruled for 53 years. He had gargantuan appetites and drank large quantities of chocolate. This tasty habit was about the only thing he had in common with his wife, Marguerite Louise d'Orleans. As a cousin of the Sun King, Louis XIV, she'd enjoyed the frivolity of court life in Versailles, where chocolate was served regularly. After she married Cosimo III in 1661, she was very demanding and hostile, leaving the Pitti Palace in a huff in 1664. Her unruly and unbecoming behavior— including swimming nude in a public river—continued until 1674 when Cosimo III finally agreed Marguerite Louise could return to France and live at the convent of Saint-Pierre de Montmartre. Beset by domestic, economic, political, and familial troubles, with poor health caused by his obesity, Cosimo demanded his physician concoct a medicine based on chocolate. He wanted a treatment for his ailments, and also a chocolate-based medicinal that could compete with Spain's monopoly.

In "Chocolate in History: Food, Medicine, Medi-Food," Donatella Lippi notes that the members of the Medici family enjoyed chocolate as food and believed in its medicinal properties.

> In a letter written by Father Ettore Ghislieri to Cardinal Leopoldo de' Medici in 1671, the former thanks the Cardinal for a box of assorted chocolates, mentioning his favorite varieties as a citron-flavored one and one based on a Spanish recipe. He also states that his doctors have endorsed chocolate as a treatment for his flatulence.[181]

Chocolate from the New World was used as medicine in *Cinquecento* Florence. Grand Duke Ferdinando I (1549–1609) took a chocolate-based medicine for his heart ailment.[182] It was medical belief at the time that chocolate could induce heart palpitations; if cinnamon and vanilla were added, these would add to its negative effects.[183] Conversely, chocolate was considered beneficial for hemorrhages, and could heal women suffering from blood loss.[184]

Florentine chocolate history acknowledges Francesco Carletti (1573–1636), a merchant who circumnavigated the globe, as the first to bring cacao to Florence. However, by 1600 his entire merchandise was plundered, so it was impossible for any of his cacao cargo to have arrived in Florence. Carletti's own account of his ordeal is vividly detailed in *My Voyage Around the World: Chronicles of a 16th Century Florentine Merchant*. Back in Florence in 1606, after twelve years of travels, he met with Grand Duke Ferdinando I and presented a remarkably comprehensive chronicle of his misadventures. He and his father sailed from Seville in 1594, and within eight years, the merchandise he'd accumulated would have made him a very wealthy man. However, after his father died on the voyage, the Portuguese ship on which Carletti was sailing was attacked near Goa (India) by corsairs from Zeeland.

The corsairs all spoke Spanish, as many were from Flanders, at that time part of the Spanish empire. Carletti understood them, and did not want to die, so he gave them the diamonds and pearls he carried. He also had 2,000 ounces of musk, and three servants, whom he also refers as slaves. Most of his slave trading had already been completed—selling people from Cape Verde in Cartagena, Colombia—so his ship also carried gold.

Carletti mentions the cacao tree and the processing of the cacao beans into chocolate. He remained in Soconusco, which he calls Sonsonate, for ten days. He left Mexico carrying "some sacks of cacao … making our way along that coast."[185] During his subsequent stops on his world voyage, he does not mention cacao or chocolate again. His main interest in trade is the slave trade, diamonds, pearls, and musk. During the attack, Carletti admits to stripping naked and offering the corsairs his own gold chain and two Catholic reliquaries, also of gold, but says "they did not want it."[186]

By the time Carletti returned to Florence in 1606, chocolate was well known there, as it was in the Kingdom of Sicily, Naples, Sardinia, and Milan. The legend of Carletti as being the one to introduce chocolate is inaccurate: the convent nuns were already selling hot chocolate by 1600, prior to Carletti's return without any merchandise whatsoever. The convent nuns in Sicily had already introduced chocolate bars in Modica—and the acclaimed nun apothecaries of Florence used chocolate as medicine.

In her essay, "The Nun Apothecaries of Renaissance Florence: Marketing Medicines in the Convent," Sharon T. Strocchia describes how nuns had prepared medicine and administered drugs since the Middle Ages. This long tradition led to the Renaissance Florentine convent pharmacies, called *spetieria,* which "capitalized on the burgeoning interest in medicinals to develop new revenue sources and enlarge their charitable scope."[187] In Cinquecento Florence, the religious movement led by Dominican priest Girolamo Savonarola, who emphasized charitable assistance, led the nun apothecaries to fulfill a core religious objective.[188] The additional factors that influenced the growth of nun apothecaries in Florence were: a population increase, insufficient apothecaries, lack of funds at the convents, the advent of printed health manuals, and the influx of drugs from the New World.[189] There were many nun apothecaries in Florence but only six of these were commercial pharmacies that could accommodate the needs of the public.

By 1517 the "nun apothecaries" were distilling herbs for sale and within a decade their stock included: syrups for coughs, oils, electuaries (medicine mixed with honey), unguents for burns and wounds, powders, pills, purgatives, and medicinal waters.[190] At that time, European medicine thought that illness was a result of an imbalance in the four humors: blood, phlegm, black bile, and yellow bile. Physicians assessed symptoms based on the qualities of heat, cold, moisture, and dryness. The medicine they prescribed intended to restore humoral balances. According to the essay, "The European Reception of the First Drugs from the New World," by J. Worth Estes, European pharmacopeia of the sixteenth century included New World medicine such as guaiac for syphilis, since it was believed that it purified the blood of poisonous humors; sarsaparilla as a cure for scabies and rheumatism; cocoa butter ointment; and tobacco to expel stomach worms.[191] The red tree sap known as *Sangre de Drago*, Dragon's Blood, from the indigenous trees of Ecuador, was painted on wounds to staunch bleeding and to seal and protect injuries.[192]

The Florentine nuns also compounded medicines tailored for individual patients, and they were clever not to compete any further with the lay apothecaries. The nuns of Santa Caterina da Siena, the first commercial nun pharmacy, did not sell wax, which was big money maker at the time: they knew this would have infuriated the monopoly held by the guild.[193] The head pharmacist at this convent was Giovanna Ginori, a close friend and confidant of the Savonarolan activist Lorenza Ginori Rucellai. Each of the convent pharmacies cultivated friendships with high-placed individuals who could help them with raw materials, contacts, and noble patrons.

The nuns were aware of market innovations at other pharmacies that were already using medicinal substances from the New World. such as the bark of the Ecuadorian *cinchona officinalis* tree. The indigenous people of southwest Ecuador, whose territory bordered the original cacao region of Chinchipe Zamora, called the bark *quina-quina* or bark of bark, and they used it to treat shivers caused by fevers. It gained much support from apothecaries when it was used to treat Louis XIV.[194]

Because of Grand Duke Cosimo III's love of chocolate, while simultaneously suffering from gout and other ailments caused by gluttony, he assigned his head physician and superintendent of the Royal Pharmacy, Francesco Redi, to concoct a proprietary remedy. Redi, who was also a poet, composed a poem in which he admits not being a proponent of chocolate as a remedy: *chocolate might not yet/be taken up or even tea, /medicines like this/ would never do for me.*[195]

FIG. 66

Nonetheless, he invented the famous jasmine chocolate that was a guarded state secret, and a success with Florentine aristocrats. Since the Florentine royals had never tasted the authentic fragrant Mesoamerican chocolate, which was made with a mixture of highly aromatic flowers, they credited Redi with an original chocolate beverage. Cosimo III gave this jasmine chocolate as a gift to foreign dignitaries, before gout ended his 53-year reign in 1723. By then his coffers were empty, and the Medici dynasty would end in 1737.

In 1743, another product from the New World was added to a restorative tonic made by the Florentine Dominican friars at the still-existent Santa Maria Novella pharmacy. It was made with the red of the cochineal insect from Mexico, and was mixed with clove, nutmeg, and orange blossom. This tonic was named "Elixir of the Medici," and was said to heal melancholy and weak hearts—but it was too late to heal Cosimo.

FIG. 67

The Duchy of Savoy in northeast Italy also has a direct connection to the history of chocolate in Europe through the 1584 marriage of Catalina Micaela, daughter of Phillip II of Spain, to Carlo Emanuel I, Duke of Savoy. Forty years prior to this royal wedding, King Phillip II—then Prince Phillip—received a momentous visit from Bishop Bartolomé de Las Casas. The Bishop brought along Maya chieftains, quetzal feathers, unique flora and fauna—and the first recorded shipment of cacao, all from Guatemala.

Initially, Catalina Micaela was not well received in the Duchy of Savoy because of what was perceived as her arrogance, including an evident desire to change the House of Savoy to reflect Spanish culture. But when Carlo Emmanuel was away at war, she served as regent, and soon earned the respect at court due to her intelligence. Nonetheless, she sent her sons to Spain for their education. She is credited to having introduced chocolate to the Duchy of Savoy, by then centered in the city of Turin.

On December 11, 1602, the Duke of Savoy attacked the city of Geneva in Switzerland. His soldiers scaled the city ramparts but the locals resisted. One woman threw down a boiling cauldron of soup and killed one soldier. The attack ended in retreat, celebrated annually in Geneva with a commemorative event called *L'Escalade*. The central element of this festivity is a large molded chocolate in the shape of the cauldron. Inside the *Marmite de l'Escalade*, as the pot is called, are vegetables made from marzipan. The locals then break the chocolate pot in tribute to the woman who defended Geneva from the Duke of Savoy.

By 1678, chocolate shops were licensed in Turin, and in 1852 an innovative chocolate spread was invented. Due to high cacao prices, a problem with supply, and an abundant supply of local hazelnuts, the chocolatiers of Turin blended milk chocolate with ground hazelnuts into a spread that was initially dubbed Gianduia, the name of a marionette character of a stereotypical Piedmont peasant. This chocolate spread later became Nutella.

Mary Tuke:
The Founder of the English
Chocolate Industry

MARY TUKE'S ERASURE FROM THE ANNALS OF ENGLISH CHOCOLATE HISTORY IS disheartening. Had it been a deliberate obliteration based on something negative she did in her lifetime (1695–1752) to make people want to forget that she single-handedly started the chocolate industry in England, then at least there would have been more archival information on her. In fact, it was her steadfast, nose to the grindstone approach to chocolate manufacture, and her modest Quaker upbringing, that faded the memory of her many accomplishments.

It's been a research challenge to discover details about this compassionate and dedicated chocolate merchant from York, England. My premature enthusiasm over the archives of the University of York's Borthwick Institute for Archives led me to other local Tuke surnames, but my hopes soon deflated. The archives did not contain any record of the woman who founded this city's famed chocolate industry.

The digital archives for the Tuke family date to 1660, and they indicate that the Tuke family owned a tea and coffee business in York.[196] They do not confirm that it was Mary Tuke who started the business in 1725, at the age of thirty. Her father died in 1704, her mother in 1723; as the eldest child, Mary had the responsibility of bringing up her siblings. The Tukes were members of the Society of Friends (Quakers) and were involved in philanthropic work linked to their Quaker faith. In particular, the Tukes founded the Retreat Asylum for the humane treatment of the mentally ill, and they were members of the Anti-Slavery Society of York.

The Quaker faith would become the common thread among the confectioners and chocolatiers of York. Their core beliefs of pacifism, austerity, sobriety and social justice, would lead them to provide better work conditions and fair wages for their employees. When Mary Tuke opened her grocery store in Walmgate, she joined many merchants serving the burgeoning mercantile city of York. Her store was near Walmgate Bar, one of the twelfth-century stone gates to this ancient city, still standing today.

In the eighteenth century, York was a market city on the river Ouse that drew trade and shoppers from the surrounding area. The local guild that controlled the docks, the trade, and the shops was the Company of Merchant Adventurers, given its authority by Elizabeth I. This was a powerful trade association, and even today, the large timber-framed Guildhall is imposing.

For years Mary Tuke refused to pay for membership to the Company of Merchant Adventurers for the right to sell chocolate, coffee, chicory, and spices from her store. The Company had initially refused her based on their rule that members must be freemen in trade. Mary Tuke was an orphan, an unmarried woman responsible for her siblings, and she rebelled against the Company's trading restrictions.[197] She adhered to the principles of her Quaker faith—simplicity, peace, integrity, community, equality, and stewardship. Living according to these principles must have given meaning to her life—and the courage to stand up to the dominant guild. Following her dignified leadership, other Quaker confectioners became chocolatiers in York reflecting their common conviction that chocolate did not contradict with a core belief in temperance.

Mary Tuke was the first chocolate shop in York, but the first chocolate shop to open in England was in London by a Parisian shopkeeper in June 1657. The advertisement placed in Needham's *Mercurius Politicus* read:

FIG. 69

FIG. 70

An excellent West India drink called chocolate, in Bishopsgate, at a Frenchman's house being the first man who did sell it in England. Ready at any time, and also unmade at reasonable rates, it cures and preserves the body of many diseases.[198]

According to authors Paul Chrystal and Joe Dickenson in their book *The Chocolate History of York*, the first English chocolatiers emphasized the medicinal and aphrodisiac qualities of chocolate. Soon chocolate shops in London opened up around Covent Garden, Pall Mall, and St. James. In 1693 Mrs. White's Chocolate House opened in Mayfair, serving luxurious chocolate to the wealthy. In Samuel Pepy's diaries of the 1660s, he writes about drinking "jocolatte," while Samuel Johnson (1709–1784) advocated drinking chocolate instead of alcohol.[199] In the 1782 novel *Cecilia* by Fanny Burney, the protagonist is presented with chocolate as a sign of prosperity. The affluent Colonel Tilney in Jane Austen's first novel *Northanger Abbey*—completed in 1803— drinks chocolate at breakfast. In William Thackeray's *Vanity Fair*, published in 1848, Rawdon Crawley carries "chocolate, which he always made and took to her of a morning," up to Becky Sharp. In *A Tale of Two Cities* by Charles Dickens, published in 1859 but set during the French Revolution, the character Monseigneur drinks prodigious quantities of chocolate. Chocolate had not only made a hit in the chocolate houses, but also in literature.

The bourgening chocolate houses in London soon became politically charged. In 1675, King Charles II tried to close down the chocolate houses in order "to quell the sedition and radical sentiments they nurtured."[200] The Cocoa

Tree Chocolate House became known as the Tory Cocoa Tree House for the political leanings of its clientele. London's chocolate houses realized a favorable business opportunity and turned their chocolate shops into private establishments for wealthy, privileged males, thereby creating the first English gentlemen's clubs.[201]

By 1725 when May Tuke opened her shop, York was going through a commercial and social transformation. The social life of the city was growing due to entertainment opportunities such as the races at Knavesmire, society balls, theatre, and coffee and chocolate for the gentry. Not only were the wealthy able to enjoy luxury items, but the working conditions for the working class were improving, many due to the Quaker business owners, and the workers had more leisure time to stroll along the promenade newly created alongside the river.

On the other hand, the ships bringing more goods into York had become too large to navigate the Ouse, and new ports were opened elsewhere. The control of trade by the Company of Merchant Adventurers of York was waning. Mary Tuke must have been aware of the changing market forces when she proceeded in her business without the approval of the Company of Merchant Adventurers. For almost eight years, they imposed fines and threatened her with imprisonment, but she persevered.[202] She focused on creating new products, and succeeded with the introduction of Tuke's Superior Rock Cocoa, a winning product composed of cocoa and sugar compressed into a cake that would dissolve in hot water. In time, the Merchant Adventurers Company admitted Mary Tuke as a member.

FIG. 71

In 1752 Mary Tuke died, leaving her business to her nephew William. He and his descendants continued the business until 1862 when they sold it to a fellow Quaker, businessman Henry Isaac Rowntree. In York, the Quaker-owned chocolate businesses were held in esteem as being trustworthy. With the prosperity created by his aunt, William Tuke founded the innovative mental asylum The Retreat. He was moved to action in 1790 after the sudden death of Hannah Mills, a young Quaker widow from the nearby city of Leeds in West Yorkshire. Her family had placed her in a mental facility because she was suffering from depression after the death of her husband. Within one month, Hannah Mills died. Her relatives had been denied visitation throughout her stay. William Tuke and the Quaker community determined that the draconian and inhumane practices had to change. Without the wealth earned by Mary Tuke, her descendants would not have had the capital to open this comprehensive mental health facility in the countryside outside York. The Retreat made psychiatric history by reshaping attitudes and treatment for the mentally ill.[203]

A Cautionary Tale of Curaçao's Cacao

*I*N JUNE 1975, I THREW CAUTION TO THE WIND AND BOARDED A DILAPIDATED CRUISE ship from Nice, France to Guayaquil, Ecuador, considered the world's first cacao port in the eighteenth century.[204] I stepped aboard the *SS Donizetti* feeling a certain malaise. I'd concluded my undergraduate degree and had loved living in France for three years, but I was reluctant to return to California and start graduate school in the fall. My outlook was the opposite of my Basque ancestor, Ojer de Velástegui, who enthusiastically joined Christopher Columbus in 1492 aboard the *Pinta* for a life-changing voyage to the New World.

The *Pinta* hit the doldrums in the Canary Islands, where it lingered for one month, but my personal lassitude at sea only lasted a few days. By the time the *Donizetti* reached Tenerife in the Canary Islands, the militant South American college students aboard the cruise ship were fired up with the revolutionary jargon that they'd learned in Soviet universities. They were heading back to their homelands ready to change the status quo.

The students turned their political ire on me, the only passenger with a passport from the United States of America, their perceived enemy country. I had to stay mentally alert for twenty-five days in order to dodge these aggressive fools. While swimming laps in the second-class pool, I apparently caught the eye of an unmarried gentleman from Curaçao, traveling in first class. He invited me to dinner with the captain, and we danced to an elegant Latin orchestra. That opulent evening was the polar opposite of time spent with the loud crowd down below in second class steerage.

Both the Captain and Mr. Curaçao were chocolate connoissieurs, and the chef had prepared a chocolate extravaganza. There were five-feet-tall molded chocolate statues of mermaids, Neptune, and seahorses, and tables replete with chocolate pastries, chocolate truffles, and oozing milk-chocolate fountains. In between chocolate servings, I told Mr. Curaçao about my unsuccessful genealogical research in the Basque country. Generalissimo Franco was still in power in 1975 and the country lived in fear of this tyrant. Furthermore, the Basque ETA rebels had a stronghold in my ancestral town of Velastegui in Guipuzcoa, and when car bombs became a daily occurrence in the region, I fled back to Paris. Mr. Curaçao listened attentively, chomped on more chocolate, and nodded with genuine empathy.

Aboard the *Donizetti* I learned significant life lessons about personal safety, political friction, and the dark side of the trans-Atlantic trade with the West Indies. My conversation with Mr. Curaçao aboard the cruise ship is permanently etched in my brain.

I decided to tell him about my failed attempts at putting together the genealogical puzzle of my Sephardic Jewish roots. The Edict of Eviction of 1492 forced all the Sephardic Jews to head for the borders or for Seville, to board ships sailing elsewhere. Many Sephardic Jews settled in Bayonne, considered the chocolate city of France, but many more went to the Netherlands, where they introduced chocolate. By 1621 they were major stockholders in the Dutch West India Trading Company. Many more Jews—like some of my ancestors—decided to convert to Catholicism, under duress, and live the life of a *converso*. (They were rudely called *marranos,* pigs.) Others, known as Crypto-Jews, secretly practiced Judaism while outwardly practicing Catholicism.

"It's a shame you didn't know me sooner, I could have resolved all your problems, just like that." Mr. Curaçao snapped his fingers and smiled so sincerely.

"But how?"

"Surely you know that everything in this world can be bought?" he snickered.

When he recognized the naïve alarm in my eyes, he changed his tune.

"That is to say, I have the connections that could have easily found the answers for you."

Now it was my turn to laugh. "Are you kidding? Do you know the number of days I've spent in dusty archives looking for information about my ancestors?"

He stroked my long hair as if I were an innocent preschooler or his favorite cat.

"Surely you know the history of Curaçao? We'll be docking there soon and I'll take you to my home, would you like that?"

He didn't wait for my answer. "We *Sefardis* have ruled all trade in Curaçao since Europe craved sugar, chocolate, and tobacco," he bragged. "We are the best problem solvers."

"But that was back in the 1600s, right?" I asked.

Instead of answering my question, he took me out on the dance floor. Between dancing boleros, tango, and cha-cha-cha, Mr Curaçao proceeded with his brief history lesson on the Sephardic Jews of Curaçao. Throughout the years, I've verified the facts and dates he cited, and to my surprise, he was fairly accurate. My subsequent interest in the cacao trade led me to add layers of information, from year to year, to Mr. Curaçao's recounting. Following is a summary of his historical perspective, with the addition of the facts that I later learned.

In 1630, Sephardic Jewish traders, expelled from Spain and Portugal, were welcomed in Bayonne, where they specialized in chocolate production. Their rise to prominence instilled envy by the local confectionaries' guild, who maneuvered to change the laws in their favor, and ousted the Jewish chocolatiers. Among the leading Sephardic Jews in the contraband trade of cacao with Spain were Jácome Luis, and Álvaro Luis. They used the port of Bayonne to traffic in smuggled cacao from Spain into Amsterdam.[205]

According to James F. Gay in "Chocolate Production and Uses in the 17th ad 18th Century North America," smuggling by the Dutch, English, and French was a major component of the supply network.[206] When the British privateer ship *Charles Mary Wentworth* captured the Spanish brigantine *Nuestra Señora del Carmen* on September 4, 1797, it took the Spaniards' large cargo of cacao.[207] In 1799 the British owner, Simeon Perkins of Liverpool, attacked a further four Spanish ships, all loaded with cacao. He sold the cargo and auctioned the captured ships.[208]

By 1761, the Jewish chocolatiers had already left Bayonne for Amsterdam or had settled throughout the Dutch West Indies. Since the mid-seventeenth century, their trade participation had been welcomed by the Dutch West Indies Company, of which many Sephardic Jews were members. The tight networks among Sephardic Jews and their extended families throughout the world of commerce, along with their involvement in the Dutch West Indies Company, enabled them to dominate the cacao business of Curaçao.[209] By 1704, the leading cacao merchant in French Martinique, D'Acosta de Andrade, had to flee to Curaçao: King Louis XIV had ordered the expulsion of all Jews from French colonies. He joined forces with a relative, Jacob Andrade da Costa, a cacao broker in Curaçao, and together their business grew.

Despite the objections of Peter Stuyvesant, Director General of the colony of New Netherland, the power of the Dutch West Indies Company prevailed: Jews were granted civil rights in Curaçao. Between 1660 and 1871, there were 200 Jewish cacao brokers operating in Curaçao.[210]

Among the brokers of this era, one woman stands out as the sole female cacao broker: Rachel Luis.[211] It is my contention that Rachel Luis was related to Álvaro Luis and Jácome Luis, the successful Sephardic Jewish cacao smugglers in Bayonne. It is very plausible that either or both men or their Luis descendants ended up in Amsterdam or in the Dutch colony of Curaçao, working in the

lucrative cacao trade. The Bayonne Luis cacao smugglers were obviously astute to the political and business fluctuations, and as cagey smugglers they must have recognized which way the wind was blowing, and followed their co-religionists to the West Indies. The surname Luis or Luiz—the letters Z and S were commonly interchangeable in Ladino—are very rare Sephardic Jewish surnames, suggesting a probable familial Luis connection.

Additionally, the timeframe could encompass three generations of Luis family members, much like the example of the D'Acosta Andrade relatives mentioned above. It's quite possible that Rachel Luis was a noteworthy cacao broker, from a family of cacao brokers. In a field of 200 brokers, only a handful of names appear in the archives, with Rachel Luis the only woman: she must have come from a family known for their cacao acumen. She may have been the widow or sister of a male Luis cacao broker, and must have handled the business with wisdom in order to earn the respect of fellow brokers.

On board the *Donizetti*, Mr. Curaçao didn't mention one word about the heinous slave trade by the Dutch West India Company nor anything about the deaths of Sephardic Jews by the Inquisition. Since that evening on the cruise in 1975, I have learned the names and fate of noteworthy Sephardic Jews in the commerce of cacao in New Spain (Mexico) who suffered at the hands of the Inquisition. In 1642, a Portuguese *converso*, Luís Nuñez Pérez, owner of a cacao retail business, was sentenced to reconciliation with the Catholic Church, and sentenced to life in prison.[212] In 1645, the cacao shop of Luis de Burgos was sequestered by the Inquisition, who kept the store even after he was released.[213] The names and their sad fates would not have interested Mr. Curaçao: he only saw the world as those who could buy whatever they want and make a profit—disregarding all else.

I tried to raise the topic with him. "But you haven't told me anything about the slave trade in the Caribbean by the Dutch West Indies Comp—"

He swatted away my question. "That's old news, don't you think?" he whispered in Ladino, as if we two and our ancestors had been coconspirators way back then.

"But chocolate and sugar were the 'it' products of years gone by. What is it that you trade in now?" I asked him.

"Whatever the world craves most."

The orchestra leader announced the last dance of the evening. Mr. Curaçao snapped his fingers and a lackey approached with a small jewelry box. He opened it and tried to clasp a luminescent pearl necklace around my neck. I declined the gift but agreed to one last dance with him.

He squeezed my waist too tightly; his fingers tapped a Morse code down my spinal column, a code that I didn't want to understand or acknowledge. When the music stopped and we walked away from the dance floor, all eyes were on us since the lackey was waiting, ramrod straight, holding another jewelry box. This time it contained a gold ring with a baguette-cut emerald. I glanced at the Neapolitan captain: he was nodding at another officer, as if they had placed a wager on my reaction to the new gift. At that instant I realized that the ship's Italian officers were somehow indebted to Mr. Curaçao; that they were somehow in cahoots with him; that Mr. Curaçao's contraband must be stowed surreptitiously on the ship —and that they all saw me as his young prey. I declined the ring firmly, and both the captain and Mr. Curaçao guffawed at my proper upbringing.

Mr. Curaçao's wolfish smile revealed more than a hint of malice. "You didn't pay attention to the moral of my story, did you?" he asked.

I said goodnight and pecked his cheek in the aloof and disengaged Parisian style I had learned to politely dismiss a man's unwanted attention.

"Oh, but surely, you know who I am?" he whispered hoarsely and clamped my arm like a vise. "Everything has its price, *mi dushi*."

This meant "my sweetheart" in his Curaçao Papiamento dialect. I spent the rest of the cruise trying to dodge him as well as the foolish revolutionary students.

Colonial USA

On September 29, 1641 a Spanish ship named *Nuestra Señora del Rosario y el Carmen* sailed right into the eye of the storm off the coast of the Bahamas. It was not the first treasure ship to set sail from Havana to Seville that same unfortunate week when the hurricane season was underway. Just the day before, the 600-ton Spanish galleon, *La Pura y Limpia Concepción,* loaded with the famous silver 8 *reales*—Pieces of Eight—ran aground on the reefs of Hispaniola. It wasn't until 1986 when an expedition found the remaining treasure from this galleon. The captain of the *Nuestra Señora del Rosario y el Carmen,* Hermenexildo López, was an experienced navigator, and in order to lighten his ship, he threw overboard as much cargo as possible. But he kept the cacao on board.[214]

Once they arrived in Saint Augustine, Florida, Captain López decided that since the crates and barrels of cacao were wet, he would store them in his temporary house. Saint Augustine was first claimed as Spanish territory in 1513 by Ponce de León, and became a permanent Spanish settlement in 1565, two decades before the English settlement in Roanoke Island, and four decades before Jamestown, Virginia.

The authorities in Saint Augustine accused Captain López of smuggling cacao. The Official Judges of the Royal Treasury of La Florida and the Governor and Captain of these provinces seized and auctioned the cacao. Among the list of persons who rightfully received their cacao shipment was the wife of M.L.Mateo, making her the first woman, on record, to own cacao in Florida.[215]

In 1670, much farther north on the eastern seaboard, two women filed petitions with the selectmen of Boston to operate a chocolate and coffee tavern.

They were emboldened to open an establishment by the success of John Hull, the first Bostonian merchant to trade in cacao and tobacco, beginning in 1667. Hull was a silversmith and mint master, and had also lost his cacao-carrying ship, the *Providence,* in a Caribbean storm near a French island.[216] In his essay "Silver Chocolate Pots of Colonial Boston," Gerald W. Ward identifies the women petitioners as Dorothy Jones and Jane Barnard. Their petition read: "To keepe a house of publique Entertainment for the selling of Coffee and Chucalettoe."[217]

Throughout the eighteenth century, there were twenty-four chocolate grinders in Boston, most of them in the city's North End. Chocolate merchants such as Mrs. Hannah Boydell offered tea, coffee, chocolate, loaf and Muscavado sugars at her shop on King Street.[218] The historic Green Dragon Tavern on Union Street, which served chocolate, was the meeting place of the St. Andrews Lodge of Freemasons. Paul Revere was a member, and he started his historic ride from this tavern. By trade he was a silversmith who crafted chocolate pots.[219]

The familial and commercial networks among Sephardic Jewish cacao and chocolate merchants in New York extend back to 1702 when Joseph Bueno de Mesquita was involved in the cocoa trade.[220] In "Nation of Nowhere," Celia D. Shapiro states that in "addition to being loyal kinsmen and excellent businessmen, the chocolate traders and merchants were part of the larger community of Jews."[221] Shapiro cites Abraham de Lucena as a key player in the colonial-era

FIG. 73

Appraisment of the Goods Wares Merchandize & Slaves
belonging to the Estate of the Late deceased. Abraham
De Lucena. Taken by Order. of his Widow & Executrix
M.rs Rachell De Lucena. In New York y.e 22.th Sept. 1725

1 Lockin Glass. 1 p.r Sconces. 1 Table. 1 beaver Carpet	£ 2..10..:-
6 Leather Chairs 2 Cain Chairs & 1 Couch. 6 Matted Chairs	.. 1..9..:-
1 p.r Andirons 4 large & 10 Small pictures. 1 Chest of draws	3..5..:-
1 Cubbord. 12 p. Earthenware. 1 Old Chest 1 Tea Tray	- - ..1..:..:-
2 Silver Spoons; w.t. 3 Ounces	- - ..1..4..:-
1 Old Chest with Buttons &. Some od things 1 Beam & 4½℔ w.ts	..2..19..:-
1 Old bed a Blankett. a Rugg & 1 old Trunk	..1..10..:-
1 Bedsteed & Callico Curtains. 1 Feather bed & beding	..4..10..:-
5 Cain Chairs. 1 Trunk. 1 Chest. 1 Box. 1 Table. 3 pictures	..1..3..:-
7 Feather Tippetts. 20 yds Silk 43 yds Worsted Stuff 20 yd linnen	} 11..19..6
Some Buttons. Fringe Laces, Spice Orris & Severall od things	
1 Chest with Some books, 1 p.r Money Scales & w.t 1 Trunk & 2 Chests	..:..19..:-
3 pewter Dishes. 12 plates. 1 Chees plate. 2 porringers 3 Basons 6 Spoons	..1..5..:-
2 Knives. 2 forks. 1 Brass pypan. 1 Iron pott. 7 p. Earthenware	..:..14..:-
1 Brass Candlestick. 1 Gridiron. 1 p.r Tongs. 1 Copper Chocalet pott	..:..6..6
1 Trammell. 1 Brass Skillet. 1 Iron pott. 1 Iron Kettle. old Tubs	..:..15..:-
One Negro Woman Called Ruth with a Young Child	
One Negro Woman Called Lucy. One Called Jenny	} all at 90..:..:—
	£: 125..9..:-

Appraised by Us.

Rob.t Lurting

W.m Harisox

chocolate business. The surname Lucena is strongly affiliated with one of the most important Jewish communities in Andalusia, Spain that dated back to the eleventh century CE. Lucena was known as a Jewish town with no gentiles.[222] Throughout the centuries, its Jewish scholars and poets were renowned. However, in 1391, the Jewish community was violently destroyed, and its citizens were forced to escape or convert.[223] The fact that the surname continued into 1655 when Moses de Lucena arrived in New Amsterdam is a testament to this family's survival.

The archives of the Colenda Digital Repository of the University of Pennsylvania contain an inventory of the 1725 estate of Abraham de Lucena, the New York City Jewish merchant and minister of Shearithi Israel. The inventory is signed by William Burnet, Robert Lurting, and Rachel de Lucena. The document notes that Rachel de Lucena "being of the Hebrew Nation was duly sworn upon the Five Books of Moses." The inventory lists the deceased's property including enslaved people.[224] Through the marriage of his descendant Rebecca de Lucena (1713–1801) and Mordechai Gomez (1688–1750), two leading chocolate merchant families of New York were linked. Dr. Noah L. Gelfand attributes the Gomez family's success in part to their longstanding Jewish mercantile practices, and their time-honored practice of cementing business ties through marriages with families from other strategic locations.[225] Daniel Gomez sent over 100 ships from New York to Curaçao, and Gomez men married brides from Curaçao and Barbados.[226]

Mordecai Gomez's first wife was Esther Rachel Campos of Jamaica. The couple had three children and were living in New York when Esther died in 1736. Five years later, Gomez married Rebecca, the youngest daughter of Abraham Haim de Lucena, and they had four children. When Gomez died in 1763, his substantial wealth was divided, as per his will, among his seven children and his widow Rebecca. The lengthy inventory described by Leo Hershkowitz in his article "Original Inventories of Early New York Jews 1682–1763" reveals that Gomez left five houses in New York's North Ward, gold, silver and money, as well as a long list of people who owed him money, from Curaçao to South Carolina, Canada, and Amsterdam. Tragically, he also left his family six enslaved persons.[227]

Rebecca was fifty years old when Mordechai died. One would assume that she did not have a financial reason to continue to work—but still, she carried on with the family's well-known chocolate business. Between 1779 and 1781, she placed advertisements in New York for the sale of chocolate at her establishment located at number 57 Nassau Street, between Commissary Butler's and the Brick Meeting.[228] On December 2, 1780, at age sixty-seven, Rebecca placed the following advertisement in New York City's *Royal Gazette:*[229] "Rebecca Gomez, at the Chocolate Manufactory, Corner of Ann and Nassau Street, has for Sale: Muscavado sugars, coffee, pepper, ginger, indigo…..Own manufactured Chocolate, warranted free from any sediments and all pure. Great allowance made to those who buy to sell again."[230]

It is evident from the large font of the headlines in her ads that Rebecca Gomez was aware of the importance of her family name: the Gomez family had a reputation for its upright character.[231] They were charitable leaders in New York City. During a smallpox scare in 1746, the New York Assembly met in Mordecai Gomez's house in Greenwich Village. Daniel Gomez translated documents from Spanish to English for the Governor and Council of New York.[232] Moses Gomez, Rebecca's son, continued the family business. Rebecca Gomez lived until age eight-eight, and is considered the matriarch of the chocolate industry in New York.

The state of Pennsylvania is known as the chocolate capital of the United States due to its globally famous chocolate companies. In the colonial era, women were engaged as retailers, producers, and suppliers of chocolate.[233] Mary Keene Crathorne Roker of Philadelphia became a young widow in September 1767 when her husband Jonathan Crathorne, owner of a mustard and chocolate mill, died suddenly. Left with a five-year-old son and a five-month-old daughter, Mary realized that as a widow she was now legally allowed to make contracts, run her deceased husband's business, pay taxes, and buy and sell property; she could also sue and be sued. According to the Adverts 250 Project, which explores the advertising in colonial America, Mary Crathorne took over the management of her deceased husband's business. She took out a lengthy and detailed advertisement on September 3, 1767 in the *Pennsylvania Gazette*. Mary was keenly aware of the value of her brand's logo, which featured a seal with three silver balls. The advertisement included a woodcut of a bottle of mustard on the left of the seal, and a brick of chocolate on the right. She was aware that her husband had already had legal difficulties with his ex-business partner over the use of the seal.[234]

Mary Crathorne wanted to protect her brand. She did not want her products to be mistaken and she wanted consumers to recognize her chocolate and mustard by the "trademark that identified the producer."[235] "All the mustard put up in bottles," she stated in the ad, "has the above stamp placed on the bottles." Similarly, "the paper round each pound of chocolate has the same stamp thereon."[236]

In the initial September 1767 ad, she requested that any outstanding payments to her be made and she asked for any outstanding debts by her husband be "properly attested, that they may be settled and paid."[237] In an ad of February 11, 1768, she offered more products for sale, adding coffee, tea, ground ginger, whole and ground pepper, allspice, oats, oatmeal, barley rice, corks, raisins, and wines from Madeira. In November 30, 1769, she placed an ad for a mustard and chocolate maker.[238]

Mary Crathorne,

BEGS leave to inform the public (and parti-cularly those that were her late husband's cus-tomers) that she has removed from the house she lately occupied in *Lætitia-Court*, to the house in which Mrs. ARIS lately lived, at the corner of the said court, in *Market-Street*, where she continues to sell, by wholesale and retail, the genuine flour of mustard, of different degrees of fineness, chocolate well manufactured and genuine, raw and ground coffee, tea, race and ground ginger, whole and ground pepper, allspice, *London* fig blue, excellent wine and cyder vinegar, oat-groats, oat-meal, barley, rice, corks, a fresh assortment of spices, domestic pickles, *London* loaf sugar, by the loaf or hundred weight, *Muscovado* ditto, choice raisins by the cag or lesser quantity, best thin shell almonds, olives and capers, with sundry other articles in the grocery way; like-wise *Madeira*, *Lisbon*, and *Fyall* Wines, in half pipes and quarter casks, and claret in bottles.

As the articles of mustard and chocolate are ma-nufactured by her, at those incomparable mustard and chocolate works at the *Globe* mill on *Germantown* road, which her late husband went to a considerable expence in the erecting, and purchasing of *Benjamin Jackson*'s part; and as she has a large quantity of choice clean mustard-seed by her, and the singular advantage of being constantly supplied with that ar-ticle, she flatters herself that, upon timely notice, she can supply any person with large quantities of the said articles of mustard and chocolate, either for exportation or for retailing again, when a good al-lowance will be made, and the same put up in any kind of package, as may best suit the buyer.

N. B. All the mustard put up in bottles has a stamp pasted on the bottles, and also the paper round each pound of chocolate has the same stamp thereon; and lest any person may be discouraged from bring-ing small quantities of mustard-seed to her, from the singular advantage already mentioned, she therefore informs those persons that may either have great or small quantities to dispose of, that she will always be ready to purchase of them, and give the highest price.——She has also two genteel eight-day clocks, *London* made, with mahogany cases, which will be disposed of at a reasonable rate.

In 1771 Mary Crathorne married Thomas Roker, not a chocolate or mustard producer. He was a known Tory during the 1776 revolution, and by 1778, the State of Pennsylvania confiscated all of Roker's and Mary's estates.[239] Just four years after the 1776 Declaration of Independence, Mary Keene Crathorne Roker died in a boating accident, and her legacy of chocolate production in Philadelphia was forgotten.

Among the most prominent Founding Fathers of 1776, three have strong links to chocolate. As early as 1739, Benjamin Franklin was selling chocolate in his Philadelphia store. George Washington loved to drink chocolate. In 1757, he ordered 20 pounds of chocolate, and three months before his death in 1799, he ordered 50 pounds of chocolate.[240] In a November 27, 1785 letter to John Adams, Thomas Jefferson wrote from Paris advising him that chocolate is a superior article for health and nourishment.[241]

Heinous Slave Trade

*E*VEN THE DELECTABLE TASTE AND SCENT OF SUPERIOR CHOCOLATE CONFECTIONS can't cover up the sinister and violent history of its forced cultivation in the cacao belt lands that circle the Earth's equator. In June 2013, I was in Bordeaux, France on a wine journey. I took a break from the lecture and walked around the center of the city. When I looked up at the buildings of the Place de la Bourse, the former stock exchange, I realized that the painful link between Bordeaux and the historical cacao plantations of Sainte-Domingue (Haiti) was much closer than their geographic distance—4,400 miles—would suggest. I'd visited Bordeaux and its famed vineyards in the 1970s, but returning years later, I noticed something shocking in the decorative architectural elements known as *mascarons*. The word *mascaron* originated from the Italian *mascheron*, and signifies a grotesque mask. The *mascarons* represent different mythical characters, or their facial expressions—opened mouths or furrowed eyebrows—depict vivid human emotions. The three thousand stone *mascarons* of Bordeaux are placed above windows or doors of the city's Baroque buildings, easily viewed from street level. The single *mascaron* that stopped me dead on my tracks was the solemn stone face of an African woman.

It impelled me to find out the meaning of her serene face among the other traditional *mascarons*. I picked up my pace and walked all around the buildings near the crescent-shaped harbor along the Garonne River, where I soon saw more African-faced *mascarons*. Bordeaux became a wealthy city in great part due to its direct participation in the slave trade of the seventeenth and eighteenth centuries. The French, like the Spanish, Portuguese, British, and Dutch, were involved in the trade of chocolate, sugar, tobacco, and other commodities, and they all relied on the forced labor of enslaved human beings, which these

FIG. 76

European powers kidnapped from Africa and brought to their plantations in the West Indies.

It's been estimated that between 1672 and 1837, 180 shipowners from Bordeaux led 480 slave trade expeditions. According to UNESCO's Slavery and Remembrance website, of the 1,381,000 enslaved persons loaded onto French slave ships, 1,165,000 survived the harsh journey.[242] Once they arrived in Saint-Domingue, they were set to work in the cacao and sugar plantations, with such inhumane conditions that the life expectancy of the enslaved workers was a mere five to six years.

According to Alex Puy in his article "French Merchant Capital and Slavery in Saint Domingue," the slave trade resulted in great profit:

> The slave economies everywhere shared similar characteristics and recurrent behavior patterns, such as high levels of profit and economic growth dependent on externally stimulated demand, and the universal absence of industrialization.[243]

The chocolate-loving Louis XV commissioned a royal square in Bordeaux that would celebrate him as the true symbol of France. Bordeaux proudly displays its economic and cultural successes through the symbols of the *mascarons*. The *mascarons* of Neptune and Mercury at the former Stock Exchange Hall represent the city's incomparable commerce. A few charming blocks away from the Place de la Bourse, one can enter two historic chocolate shops, each one more than a century old, both still producing the most exquisite chocolate confections.

On the day I visited, I saw a corner display in one shop of large molded chocolate statues of Roman mythological goddesses, surrounded by trees and floating ribbons that created a pastoral dreamland. The goddesses gracefully extended arms and demure smiles invited the customer to inhale the scent of the food of the gods, the *Theobroma cacao,* and stand in the long line to pay for their purchases of chocolate confections.

I walked back to the *mascaron* of Minerva, the goddess that protects the arts, such as the artful structure of the 1789 Grand Théâtre de Bordeaux. But I couldn't stop thinking of the way the city's African *mascarons* are silent reminders of the wealth earned through the heinous slave trade. Their passive stone faces obscure the immense pain suffered by enslaved human beings, who toiled in the harsh conditions of the Saint-Domingue plantations.

Although the African face *mascarons* will always remain symbols of the nameless victims of the slave trade, in 2019 the city of Bordeaux commissioned a life-size, figurative bronze statue of Modeste Testas (ca. 1765–1870). Modeste's birth name was Al Pouessi, and she was captured as a young girl in Ethiopia around 1779, sold to two brothers, François and Pierre Testas, who were slave traders from Bordeaux. Her full name was Maitte Adélaide Modeste Testas. She was taken by François Testas to Saint-Domingue and had two children fathered by him. Upon his death, she gained her freedom and inherited 51 acres of land there. As a condition of François Testa's will, Modeste had to marry an emancipated man named Joseph Lespérance, and together they had several children. One of her descendants, François Denys Légitime, was president of Haiti from 1888–1889. After the unveiling of Modeste's bronze statue in Bordeaux on May 10, 2019, another descendant, Lorraine Manuel Steed, made the following statement about Modeste (translated from French by the author):

"J'ose croire qu'en étant celle qui partage l'histoire des miens, il y a un but. Peut-être celui de libérer ceux qui comme moi sont emprisonnés psychologiquement par le traumatisme d'un passé que nous avons dans les veines mais que nous n'avons pas vécu."

"I dare to believe that she's the one who shares the story of my ancestors; that's her mission. Perhaps it is to free those, who like me, are psychologically imprisoned by the past trauma that we have in our veins, but which we have not lived.[244]"

✳ ✳ ✳

FIG. 77

Once the devastating diseases and atrocious working conditions decimated the indigenous people of the Americas, the Spanish brought in African enslaved persons to work the cacao, sugar and tobacco plantations. The slave ships arrived regularly, southbound along the Pacific Coast, from Panama to Lima, Peru to disembark the human cargo that would be forced to work in silver mines. One such slave ship that shipwrecked in 1553 off the Esmeraldas coast of northernmost Ecuador carried a future leader of a group of formerly enslaved persons, Alonso de Illescas. Born in Senegal and brought up by his owner in Seville, Spain, he and several other African people escaped the shipwreck on the coast of San Mateo Bay. They hid among the indigenous population further inland in the dense, swampy river tributaries of tropical Esmeraldas. Through marriage to an indigenous leader's daughter, Alonso de Illescas became the recognized leader of a group of former slaves, who declared themselves free.

According to the Report from the Rapoport Delegation on Afro-Ecuadorian Land Rights November 2009, by 1563 the Audiencia Royal—or colonial court—in Quito wanted to build a port in Esmeraldas. The authorities in Quito "looked to Afro-descendants to act as intermediaries and peacekeepers between them and the indigenous inhabitants of the area."[245] However, as an armed group, Illescas and his people were perceived as a threat to the Spanish, though Quito, in the Andean highlands, was 200 miles away and 9,500 feet higher in elevation. As Dr. Tom Cummins writes, the Illescas community of escaped slaves, Indians, and mixed race "provided a safe haven for future slaves."[246] Eventually, Illescas swore allegiance to the Spanish Crown, but he and his descendants continued to rule their domain in Esmeraldas with impunity. The Spanish Crown decided that the Illescas community "posed a lethal threat to the whole of the Viceroyalty of Peru by potentially providing safe harbor for English and Dutch marauders."[247]

The Spanish Crown kept a wary eye on the independent, indomitable, quarrelsome Afro-Ecuadorians and their multi-racial descendants, but since the cacao

FIG. 78

plantations were south of Esmeraldas, and the cacao was shipped from the port of Guayaquil, 288 miles south of Esmeraldas, the profits kept rolling in: Esmeraldas was just a backwater pain in the neck. By the mid-seventeenth century, Ecuador provided half of the cacao exported from South America. In 1599, Juan del Barrio Sepúlveda, a Spanish official in Quito, commissioned a painting of another Afro-Ecuadorian leader named Don Francisco de Arobe, and his two sons. Don Francisco, the son of an escaped African slave and an indigenous Nicaraguan woman, ruled a town of 500 people in the province of Esmeraldas.[248] The large oil-on-canvas portrait was painted by an indigenous painter Andrés Sánchez Galque, a member of the *Cofradía* of the Rosary: this was the artist guild in Quito that allowed master indigenous artists as members. The men in the painting wear Spanish ruffs and doublets, as well as Andean fabrics, and gold nose and ear piercings; all three brandish spears. Dana Leibsohn and Barbara E. Mundy suggest that this painting reveals that while Don Francisco agreed to be a subject of Philip III of Spain, his stance and his military readiness show that he is "hardly the defeated."[249] Based on the proud confidence—and apparent affluence—of these three Afro-Ecuadorian chieftains, and the number of people they led, one would expect economic growth in Esmeraldas, similar to the incredible cacao growth in the bordering provinces.

Rather than economically develop Esmeraldas, the cacao producers concentrated on the Guayas Rivers basin south of Esmeraldas for the cultivation of the desirable *arriba nacional* cacao. They used the traditional river routes to transport the cacao to the port of Guayaquil, where many landowning families had vast agricultural properties, many founded in the colonial era. These large landowners relied on a system of debt servitude known as *concertaje*. Although this was officially abolished in 1906, many landowners still used this type of servitude to dramatically reduce labor costs. In "Cocoa, Finance and the State in Ecuador, 1895-1925," Paul Henderson describes the instrumental role of the railway in the plantation system. By 1872, the Guayaquil to Quito railway, a feat of engineering, created not only an additional mode of transportation for cacao shipments: it also enabled transportation of impoverished indigenous workers from the highlands.[250]

However, Ecuador was to lose its dominance in the world cacao trade. The 1912–1914 Ecuadorian Civil War began when the Esmeraldas Province rose up against the central government, destabilizing the nation. By the early 1920s, cacao plant diseases such as Witches Broom and Monilia Pod Rot destroyed the cacao groves, and Ecuador faced a terminal decline in cacao production.[251]

In today's coveted artisanal chocolate commerce, the *arriba nacional* cacao variety from Ecuador remains the most desired of all the international cacao for its supreme fragrance and taste profiles. Local cacao growers and international chocolate producers specifically credit the province of Esmeraldas for its *arriba nacional* cacao. In 2010, Eduardo Borrero, the trade commissioner of Ecuador in Los Angeles, stated: "Ecuadorian chocolate is organic, sustainable, fair trade, superior in quality and when Americans discover they can drastically reduce their carbon footprint by cutting out the 'middleman' they will take a serious look at the label for the word 'Arriba' before their next chocolate purchase."[252]

Irene Caselli, a journalist for BBC News, filed a report on Esmeraldas in June 2013. It is one of the poorest provinces in Ecuador, and local farmers are now incentivized by receiving more money to produce high-quality cacao. However, it appears that the Afro-Ecuadorian descendants of the bold freemen of Esmeraldas are not among those benefiting from the growth in cacao production. The European and American chocolate producers tout the uniqueness of the Esmeraldas coastal cloud forest as one of the most significant rainforest ecosystems in the world. These companies want to align themselves with Esmeraldas farmers who produce the *arriba nacional* cacao. However, for Afro-descendants from the province, the prospects for economic growth, particularly in the cacao trade, are bleak at this time, despite pressure on the Ecuadorian government to facilitate, regularize and guarantee land title for rural Afro-Ecuadorian communities in Esmeraldas.[253]

Jargon from voluminous reports and continuous international lawsuits also obscure the fact that cacao-producing countries in West Africa continue to allow reprehensible child labor practices. As recently as February 12, 2021, the human rights firm International Rights Advocates (IRA) launched legal action against the world's biggest chocolate companies. They accused the corporations of aiding and abetting the illegal enslavement of thousands of children on cocoa farms in their supply chains.[254] This was the first time a class action suit has been filed against the cocoa industry in a US court.[255] However, on June 17, 2021, the U.S. Supreme Court justices ruled, 8 to 1, in the industry's favor:

> In the end, the justices decided companies were not, in fact, legally liable for what happened in Ivory Coast—even though it appeared to constitute a form of child slavery, which is outlawed internationally. The key weakness, they said, was that the case failed to show that a lot of the business decisions leading to child labor happened on U.S. soil.[256]

For child-labor activists, the ruling was a huge blow; the IRA legal team intends to re-present the lawsuit. In a 2020 report, the U.S. Department of Labor estimates that 1.56 million children worked in the cacao farms of Ghana and the Ivory Coast, which supply a large portion of the world's cocoa.[257] Twenty years after the 2001 establishment of the Harkin-Engel Protocol to tackle child slavery in the cocoa industry, the "cocoa industry have failed to meet that goal."[258] The facts support the overwhelming reality that children are working in slave conditions in the cocoa industry, yet the recent U.S. Supreme Court ruling is daunting.

Carol Off, the author of *Bitter Chocolate: The Anatomy of an Industry,* sadly concludes: "The true history of chocolate was written in blood and sweat of countless generations of people…and there is little likelihood that this ancient and enduring injustice will be corrected."[259]

Chocolate Targets a Female Demographic

$\mathcal{I}$N THE LATE NINETEENTH CENTURY, MOTHERS IN THE DEVELOPED COUNTRIES OF Europe and North America became the target advertising demographic of the chocolate companies. By then, the chocolate industry had undergone manufacturing advances that increased production. The use of innovative industrial machines facilitated the creation of new chocolate bars and chocolate bonbons. Chocolate manufacturers in the United States and Europe quickly ascertained that children's consumption of cocoa and chocolate candy was determined by the mothers who purchased the treats—so their marketing campaigns began to be directed at women.

In Emma Robertson's book *Chocolate, women and empire: A social and cultural history,* she describes the way cocoa advertising was dominated by images of housewives and mothers.[260] In Britain, the Rowntree company—which bought Mary Tuke's company from her heirs in 1862—acknowledged targeting its marketing and advertising to mothers and wives. Rowntree had determined that more cocoa was drunk in families, and since the woman was the family's purchasing agent, she "might be inspired to act in her husband's and children's interest."[261] Rowntree's data indicated that cocoa "was shown to be the tool of both the devoted mother (a demonstration of maternal love), and the savvy housewife (economical, efficient, nutritious)."[262] Their "devoted mother" advertisements continued into the World War II era.

During wartime, the chocolate advertisers still targeted mothers, but now the ads claimed that the "vitamins in the cocoa would protect their children."[263] In fact, Rowntree claimed that "for growing children, there's no better drink at mealtimes," and that their cocoa had "more bone and muscle than ordinary cocoa."[264] The adorable children who'd appeared in the previous ads were slowly

FIG. 79

replaced by women models. In some of the ads, these women were depicted in typical gender roles, and the message of the whole campaign was that working outside the home was not good for women. "Rowntree's Cocoa advertisements therefore give us an insight into the pressures on women to return to their roles as housewives following the war and the ways in which society viewed working women."[265]

The content of the advertisements did not reflect the reality of women employed by Rowntree and other chocolate companies. Emma Robertson notes that women were employed at Rowntree since its early days; by 1904, there were 1,107 women employees. As an employment benefit, young female workers were allowed to continue their general education one day each week at what was known as Girl's Day Continuation School, managed by the company.[266] By 1912, married women were hired as temporary or seasonal staff. In 1959, Rowntree began an evening shift for married women, known as the "housewives' shift," since the women began work after they completed their housework and child care duties.[267] Well into the 1970s, women worked primarily with women in what were termed as tasks that used a woman's natural skills: handling delicate confectionery

FIG. 80

quickly, working in the card box department, piping designs onto the chocolates, and packing assortment boxes.

In 1910, at the McDonald Candy Company in Salt Lake City, Utah—almost 5000 miles from the Rowntree Company of York—young female workers went on strike, demanding better wages and improved working conditions. Many of the majority female workers at McDonald Candy Company were daughters of working-class English immigrants to Utah. Although they were not politically savvy, the striking workers managed to organize the Chocolate Dippers' Union of Utah, the first union of women workers in Utah. Some of the strikers were twelve-year-old girls who had been working full-time as chocolate dippers.

Dr. Kathryn L. MacKay, in her article "Chocolate Dippers' Strike of 1910," describes how chocolate dipping was considered a skilled job. In order to achieve the desired chocolate ridges and curls on each piece, the chocolate dipper used her fingers and wire forks and dipped them in pools of chocolate that were kept at melting point. An experienced chocolate dipper could dip 60 pounds of chocolates per day, with the fastest accomplishing from 115 to 120 pounds per day.[268]

Candy making in that era, MacKay contends, was socially acceptable paid work for women. The 1914 U.S. Census Bureau reported that 2,391 candy factories throughout the United States employed 53,658 workers, and that women accounted for 60 percent of the workforce. She adds that while advertisements

FIG. 81

depicted the eating of candy as a feminized activity enjoyed by white, middle-class women, the reality was that candy was produced by working-class women working long hours for low wages in uncomfortable conditions.[269] The female chocolate dippers at the McDonald Candy Company worked on messy, sticky floors and stairs, and their hands and nails were constantly dirty. They did their own cleaning and worked 9 to 12 hours per day. Nonetheless, their union did not last and all the strikers lost their jobs. In 1969, the McDonald Candy Company was bankrupted.[270]

In the same year as the McDonald Candy Company strike, Teresa Amatller i Cros (1878–1960) inherited the famed Catalan chocolate brand Chocolate Amatller of Barcelona. She was the last generation of the Amatller family to own the company, founded by her ancestor in 1797.

Everything about Teresa's long, long life was luxurious, grandiose, and pampered. It's been my obsession to visit Barcelona every couple of years for the last fifty years, where I always visit the iconic Sagrada Familia Basilica, as well as pay homage to Antoni Gaudí's other incomparable architectural feats. From high up on Gaudi's Casa Battló, I look out at Teresa Amatller's Barcelona house next door—the art nouveau Casa Amatller, designed by architect Josep Puig i Cadafalc. Its distinct tiered gable at the top of the façade is said to resemble a chocolate bar.[271] These two landmark houses, part of a row of late nineteenth-

FIG. 82

and early twentieth-century buildings, are located on the Passeig de Gràcia. (The street is dubbed the Illa de la Discordia, or the bone of contention, due to the incongruous architectural designs of adjacent buildings.) The fireplace mantle at Casa Amatller displays a magnificent bas-relief by renowned sculptor Eusebi Arnau i Mascort: it depicts the bow of a ship on which sit the emotive figures of an Aztec princess and a European princess who represent the chocolate trade from its origins in the Americas to its manufacture in Barcelona.

Teresa's wealth and privileged single life protected her from any quotidian concerns about neighbors, family, house repairs, or business matters. Everything in her life was managed by professionals, and she could dedicate herself to enjoying the delicacies of her chocolate empire and to collecting art. Her father, Antoni Amatller i Costa (1875–1910), shielded her from any pain or suffering after his wife, Càndida Cros y Circuns, abandoned him and four-year-old Teresa in 1882. Teresa grew up into an entitled woman who later in life created a foundation, the Instituto Amatller de Arte Hispánico, to support art historical research from medieval to modern times.[272]

Teresa's genuine interests were art appreciation and art collection, which she had learned from her father, traveling together throughout Europe, Morocco, Egypt and Tunisia. When he died in 1910, she was thirty-seven. She wanted to hold on to their joint dedication to art as a way of paying tribute to her beloved father, the only parent she had really known. Teresa understood the power of art to create an identifiable brand image and an idealized feminine presentation of their chocolate products to the buying public. She firmly believed that through the artistic graphic display of their products, human behavior could be influenced. Without ever having studied advertising, Teresa decided the promotion of the Amatller Chocolate brand should feature young, idealized women, to engage the buying public and increase sales.

Her father was an admirer of the famed Czech artist Alphonse Mucha (1860–1939), whose poster art benefitted from the creation of large lithographic printing machines. Mucha's posters were plastered throughout Paris, and became instantly recognized Art Nouveau illustrations that showed the rich texture of fin-de-siècle Paris. Mucha's posters featured beautiful women with long tendrils of hair and flowing garments surrounded by the Art Nouveau decorative botanical motifs in delicate shades of peach, gold, ochre, and *eau de Nil*.[273] "In Mucha's designs, the image of a woman was used strategically as a medium for communication, first to draw potential consumers' attention with her feminine beauty and then to send an alluring message about the product she was representing."[274]

When Antonio Amatller saw an 1897 Mucha poster of the French brand Chocolate Idéal from the Compagnie Française des Chocolats et Thés, he immediately hired Mucha through his Parisian printing and publisher F. Champenois Imprimeur-Éditeur. Mucha modified his existing designs, such as the one titled *Rêverie* or dream, and added the words Chocolate Amatller Barcelona. By 1898

FIG. 83

Mucha's vibrant posters advertising the Amatller chocolate products were viewed throughout Spain.

Teresa followed her father's footsteps in using distinctive illustrations in company advertising. In 1914, she sponsored an art competition for graphic artists. The finalists were all Spanish artists whose art reflected the Barcelona modernist aesthetic, in particular, the poster by Rafael de Penagos. The Amatller ad still had a feminine character, but the model's clothing—and hairstyle— was chic and modern, appealing to the aspirations of the contemporary female city dweller in Spain. To the present day, both the Mucha and the de Penagos graphic art is still used for Amatller chocolate brand products, and although both images are outmoded, their retro looks emphasize the longevity and authenticity of the Amatller chocolate brand. Based on the vast number of annual visitors to the Casa Amatller in Barcelona, the Art Nouveau motif of their chocolate product packaging still has cultural currency.

What did not stand the test of time in the chocolate advertising world were the giant molded chocolate statues by the Maillard Company of New York, exhibited at 1893 World's Columbian Exposition in Chicago. These supersize chocolate statues of the mythological Minerva and Venus de Milo attracted throngs to their pavilion. The chocolate statues were another oversize expression of the immigrant dreams of Henry Maillard (1816–1900). He'd arrived from France and set up his chocolate manufacturing plant in Lower Manhattan in

FIG. 84

1844. His chocolates were featured at President Lincoln's inaugural ball, but Maillard wanted to impress the chocolate world at the World's Columbian Exposition.

In his pavilion located in the Agricultural Hall, he included a chocolate statue, almost eight feet in height, of Christopher Columbus. But he believed that his chocolates had to attract a female audience, so hammered that point by displaying two giant Roman goddesses. Minerva is considered the sponsor of arts, trade, and strategy, and Venus de Milo is a symbol of female beauty. Each of these chocolate statues weighed 1,500 pounds, and towered over visitors.

Maillard's chocolate statues did not survive the fair intact: they melted in the heat and chunks of them were eaten. But the message that the appeal of chocolate and its target demographic is feminine continues to this day.

Baci: Italian Kisses

LUISA SPAGNOLI (1877–1935) HAD AN ENTREPRENEURIAL SPIRIT AND INGENIOUS mind, and her incomparable drive created a chocolate dynasty in Perugia, Italy. Her success was not easily predicted given her modest family background as the daughter of a simple fishmonger, Pasquale Sargentini.

Luisa's inquisitive character led her to learn from her city's surroundings, as well as from the proud collective history of the people of Perugia. She must have walked many times under the Etruscan Arch of the Augustus Gate, one of the eight gates of ancient Etruscan Perusia, now known as the hill city of Perugia. As a student, Luisa learned about the pre-Roman Etruscan people (8th to 5th century BCE) whose artefacts have been found in Perugia, including bronze mirrors, fine gold jewelry, terracotta sculpture, and distinctive pottery. She would have been familiar with the imposing iron statue of the mythical griffon, the mascot of the city, that stood as protector to the entrance of the Palazzo Nuovo del Popolo, the new Palace of the People, where the medieval guild members met. Luisa, like every young student from Perugia, knew that the griffon—half-eagle and half-lion—is associated with strength, courage, and intelligence,. She shared the same three characteristics.

The pride of the ordinary citizen of Perugia extended to the fame of the Renaissance artist Pietro Vannucci, better known as Pietro Perugino. Everyone knew that he'd served as an apprentice alongside Leonardo da Vinci and Filipino Lippi, and later taught Raphael. But not every citizen was able to see Perugino's masterwork mural inside the hall of the money changers (Sala delle Udienze del Collegio del Cambio) in Perugia.

In the nineteenth century, Perugia was an increasingly independent city. Though it had been brutally suppressed after the insurrection against temporal

FIG. 86

papal authority in 1859, the citizens maintained their sense of collective strength. The province gained independence from papal control after the unification of Italy in 1871.

By the time Luisa married Annibale Spagnoli, at the turn of the century, Perugia was a thriving center. In 1899 it had installed a tram that began at the top of the hill, in the historic center of town, and traveled almost two miles down to the railway station. A new theatre, the Teatro Turreno, was open, along with new chocolate shops. Coffee shops such as Caffè Falci and Caffè Medio Evo were popular, and the Pasticceria Sandri, opened in 1860 and still in operation today, was known for its exquisite deserts and beverages. The young Luisa and Annibale Spagnoli were emboldened by the commercial success around them and decided to open a *drogheria*—the unique Italian style of grocery store selling herbs, lozenges, spices, legumes, dried fruit, hot chocolate, coffee, tea, and desserts.

Luisa's natural beauty and outgoing personality drew many customers to their *drogheria*. It would have looked similar to the Antica Spezieria e Drogheria Bavicchi (Antique Spice and Drugstore Bavicchi), in business since 1897: there, one can still admire the dark wood shelves, numerous glass jars, and the sacks of beans and lentils, in every size and color. Luisa had a talent for selecting products to highlight in her shop. She filled jars with sweets such as licorice, anise and herbal candies, including honey candies for a sore throat. She promoted the traditional sugar-coated almonds, known as confetti, and given in groups of five in the traditional way: this wished newlyweds five gifts—many children, happiness,

FIG. 87

health, longevity, and wealth. She understood the marketing gimmick of reminding customers that life is both bitter and sweet, so to enjoy life while they could.

By 1907, Luisa and Annibale Spagnoli partnered with Giovanni Buitoni, and launched a chocolate candy retail business named Perugina, located it in the historic center of town. Luisa raised her sons and worked in the chocolate store. World War I began, with Italy entering the war on the side of the Entente, with Great Britain and France, and against the Triple Alliance of Germany and Austria-Hungary.[275] Annibale Spagnoli and the men of Perugia went off to war. Luisa wasted no time in keeping the business afloat, hiring women to work along with her. She understood the extra burdens placed on women in the work place, and she created "lactation rooms" for nursing mothers and day care centers for her employees.[276]

Luisa's ingenious mind resulted in the creation of the iconic chocolate *baci,* kisses, still produced and sold world-wide. Luisa came up with the recipe comprised of a few ingredients: a double coat of melted dark chocolate; roasted hazelnuts, some crushed for the Gianduia

FIG. 88

filling and the best positioned on top of each candy; and Madagascar vanilla for aromatic flavor. Initially she named this chocolate candy Cazzoto, which means a punch, but later changed its name to kisses.

By 1922, when she created the Baci Perugina brand, Luisa Spagnoli was forty-five-years-old, deep in an illicit love affair with business partner Giovanni Buitoni, fourteen years her junior. Her marriage and family life suffered, but she put all her energy into the advertising and marketing of the Baci chocolates. First, the image of a punch was changed to a passionate kiss inspired by the 1859 painting *Il Bacio* (*The Kiss*) by the Venetian painter Francesco Hayez. The oil painting by Hayez features a couple from the Middle Ages locked in a passionate kiss, their facial features obscured. The light that comes in from the left of the picture highlights the couple's embrace.[277] The shadows on one side underscore "danger and conspiracy."[278] The man's chocolate brown cape forms a wide triangle, topped by his cap: in color and shape, this suggests the hazelnut of the Baci. Luisa handcrafted the initial Baci chocolates and she wrapped love notes around them to test them with employees. These love notes were such a huge success with staff that Luisa decided to include them in the retail Baci. The range of love notes is vast, but the wording is brief. Following is an assortment of Perugina's love notes:[279]

Love, indefinable love!
G. Casanova

I understand thy kisses and thou mine.
W. Shakespeare

Lovers can live on kisses and water.
English proverb

With your kisses have I painted my starry sky.
Anonymous

Till I loved, I did not live enough.
E. Dickinson

Passion dazzles lovers. Love unites them forever.
Anonymous

Day by day and night by night we were together – all else has long been forgotten by me.
W. Whitman

Grow old along with me; the best is yet to be.
G. Sand

Before introducing the Baci to the public, Luisa hired artist Federico Seneca (1891–1976) to design the now-famous silver wrapping and Baci logo. He'd studied at the Regio Instituto di Belle Arti in Urbino and began his career making posters. During World War I he joined the Italian alpine troops and became a pilot.

Seneca employed his futuristic art style, and turned the couple kissing into a shadowy couple set against a blue background, along with the bold font with the work Baci. He remained the supervisor of advertising at Perugina until 1933.

Luisa did not rest on the success of the iconic pair of lovers of the Baci Perugina brand that was soon sold internationally. In search of a less expensive alternative to cashmere, she bred long-haired angora rabbits in order to use their silky yarn for knitwear, and she trademarked her label l'Angora Spagnoli. Today the fashion label Luisa Spagnoli continues, with more than 100 shops worldwide and headquarters in Perugia.

Luisa was a trailblazer in the chocolate industry of Italy and also in its fashion sector. The Nestlé company owns the Perugina brand today. Following are the remarkable facts about the Baci Perugina brand started by Luisa Spagnoli:[280]

- 1,500 Baci® Perugina® are made every minute.
- 55 countries import Baci® Perugina®.
- 500 million Baci® Perugina® are sold every year.
- If you lined up all the Baci® Perugina® ever sold they would circle the Earth 10 times.

Chocolate's Paradox

MY PASSION FOR CHOCOLATE STARTED WITH THE UNFORGETTABLE, MULTI-SENSORY, daily ritual of eating shaved dark chocolate with my grandfather. Like the dogs of Pavlov's experiment, as a youngster I also salivated with the joyous anticipation of my chocolate treat to come. My eardrums vibrated eagerly once the morning bells pealed at eight from the tall belfry of Quito's *Basilica del Voto Nacional*—the Basilica of the National Vow, the largest neo-Gothic basilica in the Americas. The bells' dulcet sound meant that my grandfather had left the seven a.m. Catholic Mass and would be walking home, up the steepest of hills in the already hilly Andean capital that is almost 10,000 feet above sea level. My mouth watered knowing that soon we would be served our chocolate-centric breakfast in the garden overlooking the basilica.

We cherished our large family estate that bordered the basilica because different generations of our family had witnessed the continuous construction of the basilica since 1887. To hear the bells ringing—or perhaps more significantly, the sound of the stone masons' constant hammering of new stone gargoyles of Galapagos tortoises—made us all giddy for our ongoing future. For it was said that the day the construction of the basilica ended would also be the end of the world.

The multi-sensory chocolate breakfast ritual of my childhood took a connoisseur's slow pace. My grandfather used a Swiss knife to shave slender tendrils of chocolate, along with an equal-size slice of Spanish Manchego cheese. He made me inhale both delicacies before gently placing them in my mouth. He dipped an Italian almond biscotti in the *mancerina*-style cup of hot Amatller chocolate, and taught me how to eat the biscotti in the manner of a proper young lady. He threw biscotti crumbs to the vibrantly colored birds flitting around our

FIG. 89

FIG. 90

garden pergola, such as the crimson Vermilion Flycatcher or the emerald and luminescent Sapphire-Vented Puffleg, both rarely seen in Quito today. Sated after our chocolate feast, we would stretch our legs and listen to a concert of high-pitched bird song, accompanied by the bass notes of stone carving.

My grandfather belonged to a particular generation of educated gentlemen with eccentric hobbies, not unlike the nineteenth-century owner of the Amatller Chocolate company in Barcelona and his collection of Roman archaeological glass. In 1957, when I was sharing our *chocolatadas*—our chocolate feasts—with my grandfather, he was already eighty years old. He considered himself a forward-thinking man, believing that he would undoubtably make it to one hundred years of age, and fill his ample house with taxidermy of unique Ecuadorian creatures—goals he accomplished by his centennial celebration.

Although my grandfather displayed the typical *machismo* of his era, he was first and foremost a courteous, respectful gentleman. He certainly would have disapproved of current advertising by big chocolate corporations, including Belgian companies, whose ads blatantly objectify women. According to the article, "How Women Are Portrayed in Chocolate Advertising," chocolate advertisements use women to show that eating their brand of chocolate can fulfill sexual desires and suggest the high-class value that comes along with their specific brands of chocolate.[281]

Through their print and television ads, chocolate companies promote the idea that eating chocolate will satisfy a wide range of emotions, from insecurity to sexual desire.[282] Professor Peter Rogers of the University of Bristol explains that chocolate consumption creates ambivalent attitudes in women since the ads make chocolate "highly desired" that should also "be eaten with restraint."[283] However, in "The secrets behind advertising chocolate to women and why it's about to change forever," Phil Hilton concludes that although chocolate is "one of the most pleasurable, inexpensive, guilt-laden, fetishized food stuffs," the modern woman will be in charge of her sugar consumption and take control of her calorie burn when eating chocolate.[284]

Nutritionists explain that a healthy relationship with all foods is important to mind and body. This advice is particularly vital since 45 percent of women in the United States admit to having chocolate cravings, and 91 percent of female college students crave it too. Johns Hopkins nutritionist Diane Vizthum recommends that women stop making chocolate taboo and instead to enjoy it with purpose and intention, particularly due to the health benefits of dark chocolate.[285] Kris Gunnars asserts that dark chocolate "is loaded with nutrients that can positively affect your health."[286] A 100-gram bar of dark chocolate with 70 to 85% cocoa contains manganese, magnesium, iron, copper, potassium, phosphorous, zinc and selenium. It is also loaded with antioxidants such as polyphenols, flavanols and catechins. Gunnars cites controlled studies that demonstrate how dark chocolate can improve blood flow and lower blood pressure, and very significantly, reduce the risk of heart disease.[287] Additionally, dark chocolate may reduce the risk of stroke in women.[288] My scientifically inclined grandfather would have rejoiced knowing that today's scientists are proving that dark chocolate is good for one's health. He would have said, "*Las cosas claras y el chocolate espeso,*" an idiomatic expression that means that one should keep all the facts clear and evident, but the hot chocolate always thick.

What these studies on chocolate's health benefits don't mention is that organic dark chocolate will cost the consumer more, and therefore only prosperous people from prosperous nations will enjoy the health benefits. The mass market low-quality chocolate candy will not only *not* provide health benefits, but will increase demand, leading to pressure on the supply chain. According to Bloomberg, chocolate was a $100 billion business in 2020. Yet the industry is complicit with human misery and environmental destruction in the Ivory Coast and Ghana, where 70% of the world's cacao is now produced.

Chief among the problems of human suffering is the forced child labor that continues with impunity, despite international agreements, local laws, and certifying agencies. It is a bleak and complicated problem that plagues the chocolate industry. There is a glimmer of hope that through the collaboration of advocacy groups such as Be Slavery Free, INKOTA, Green America, Mighty Earth and Wildlife Federation, there will be solutions to the problems of human exploitation and environmental degradation.

Just as the world has recently witnessed the unbelievable discoveries of the new mammal, the teddy-bear like *olinguito,* and the new frog from the *Pristimantis sira* family of jumping frogs, both from the Amazonian rainforests of Ecuador and Peru, we must remain optimistic with the advancements in the chocolate industry. As recently as July 14, 2021, researchers from the University of Bath, the University of the West of England, and Surrey Business school announced that they have proven a method that uses a DNA biomarker technique in chocolate products: this can trace cacao in a finished bar to specific cacao farms. With this low-cost method, chocolate producers will be certain that they are using cacao from farms that have approved labor and environmental standards.[289] According to Michael Rogerson, researcher at the University of Bath School of Management, this "has the potential to revolutionize sustainability in a market rife with environment and human misery."[290]

Today's chocolate bar continues to be wrapped in a millennia-old paradox. It can nourish, heal, and celebrate our lives; but, in our insatiable quest to savor more of this food of the gods, we continue to cause human suffering. Throughout chocolate's history, women have lived with this paradox: they were branded on their faces for chocolate larceny, and they got their revenge by adding poison to the hot chocolate served to their abusers. On the other hand, the ancient women cultivators and preparers of chocolate understood the value of its ritual significance to their cultures, and the women chocolate traders perservered

FIG. 91

FIG. 92

despite horrific obstacles, such as being victims of rape on the trade routes or losing their land to invaders.

However, through the example of the ingenious Catholic cloistered nuns, who became chocolate confectionaries par excellence, the chocolate industry is still indebted to female ingenuity with chocolate. We must also acknowledge that the *infantas,* the royal daughters of the Spanish Kings, arrived as brides at numerous noble courts in Europe, and introduced the chocolate drinking craze that took over the continent. Today's statistics reveal that the top five countries for international chocolate consumption are still all European. Switzerland leads the chocolate pack with a whopping 19.4 pounds of chocolate consumption per capita.[291]

My grandfather admired all things European: music, scientific findings, architecture, literature— and chocolate. I now recognize the irony of his preference for European chocolate that was made with our own exported Ecuadorian cacao beans, but he waxed poetic about the flavor profile, the texture, and the floral scents of Belgian chocolate, in particular.

He was such a Europhile that it would not have surprised him to know that it was a Belgian woman who made a small but significant addition to chocolate production. In 1915, Louise Agostini designed an elegant gift box that would prevent the chocolate pralines created by her husband, Jean Neuhaus Jr. of Brussels, from getting crushed. This box was known as the "ballotin," and was the precursor to today's ubiquitous box of chocolates. On Valentine's Day 2021, 36 million boxes of chocolate were sold in the United States.[292] Without the fearless female entrepreneurs from centuries past, who against all odds created delectable recipes, memorable brands and innovative packaging that still exist to this day, we may not have had the chance to taste so much melt-in-the-mouth, delicious varieties of chocolate.

Image With Rights Granted

CHAPTER 1

Fig. 1

Lion monkey and condor, native to Chile and Ecuador, from 'Le Costume Ancien et Moderne', Volume II, plate 1, by Jules Ferrario, engraved by Gallo Gallina (1796-1874), published c. 1820-30a (color litho)

The Stapleton Collection/Bridgeman Images

Fig. 2

Young crested capuchin monkey steals a cacao fruit.

Istock Images

Fig. 3

Ecuadorian Tsachila tribe member seen wearing traditional clothes during Kasama celebrations at Chiquilpe village in Santo Domingo. Tsachila means "true people."

REUTERS/Alamy Stock Photo

Fig. 4

Morpho peleides butterfly on leaf.

Istock

Fig. 5

CHAPTER 2

Cocoa pod crop in a chocolate production farm field.

Fig. 6

Istock

Fig. 7

Belize, Punta Gorda.

Alamy

Fig. 8

Chichen Itza Kukulkan temple pyramid, Mexico

Kravka/Alamy Stock Photo

Fig. 9

Fresco of Poor Clares in Choir.

World History Archive/Alamy Stock Photo

Fig. 10

Women sorting beans of cacao in front of a public
notice against the child labor. Ivory Coast, Côte d'Ivoire

André Quillen/Alamy Stock Photo

CHAPTER 3

Fig. 11

El Rio de Luz (The River of Light), 1877. Oil on canvas.

Frederic Edwin Church

American, 1826-1900

National Gallery of Art

Fig. 12

Theobroma cacao. Jakarta

Jan Brande, November 1783

Dutch

Rijksmuseum, Amsterdam

Fig. 13

Karajia coffins, near Chachapoyas, Peru

Maxime Dube/Alamy Stock Photo

Fig. 14

Shuar Territory, Amazon, Ecuador

Mark Fox/Alamy Stock Photo

Fig. 15

Indigenous man on typical wood canoe chopped from a single tree. Navigating murky water of Ecuadorian Amazon primary jungle.

Ammit/Alamy Stock Photo

Fig. 16

Shrunken Head of the Shuar People of South America. Steve Vidler/ Alamy Stock Photo

Fig. 17

Shuar Territory, Amazon, Ecuador.

Mark Fox/Alamy Stock Photo

Fig. 18

Pre-Columbian art. Valdivia culture. Ecuador. 3500 BC-1800 BC. Venus statuette. 8 x 12,5 cm. From Ecuador. Private collection. Bridgeman Images

Fig. 19

Guayaquil, Ecuador. Museo Antropológico y de Arte Contemporano

Prime by Dukas Presseagentur GmbH/Alamy Stock Photo

Fig. 20

Amazonian woman blowing into dart gun.

Sunshine Pics/Alamy Stock Photo

Fig. 21

"Relacion historíca del viaje a la Americana Meridional, 1748.

Smith Archive/Alamy Foto de Stock

Fig. 22

Temple I – Temple of Ah Cacao

Temple of the Great Jaguar

Tikal, Guatemala, Alamy Images

CHAPTER 4

Fig. 23

Maya culture performance "Los Rostros de Ek Chuah," honoring the god of cacao. Xcaret Park, Riviera Maya, Mexico.

Greg Vaugh/ Alamy Stock Photo

Fig. 24

Choc Mol

Chichen Itza, Mexico

Alamy Images

Fig. 25

Tzotzil women at the village of Oventic, Chiapas, Mexico, August 9, 2003. Many supporters of the rebel Zapatista National Liberation Army (ESLN) wear masks to conceal their identities.

REUTERS/Alamy Stock Photo

Fig. 26

Xalapa Museum, Veracruz, La Venta, Mexico

914 Collection/Alamy Stock Photo

Fig. 27

The Dresden Codex, is a pre-Columbian, Maya book of the eleventh of twelfth century of the Yucatan Maya in Chichén Itza

World History Archive/ Alamy Stock Photo

Fig. 28

Codex Fejérváry-Mayer depicts specific aspects of the *tonalpohualli,* the sacred 260-day Mesoamerican augural cycle. The painted manuscript divides the world into five parts. T-shaped trees delineate compass points.

Science History Images/ Alamy Stock Photo

Fig. 29

Princeton University Art Museum

The Princeton Vase, A.D. 670–750

Late Classic

Maya ('Codex' style)

Ceramic with red, cream, and black slip, with remnants of painted stucco

Museum purchase, gift of the Hans A. Widenmann, Class of 1918, and Dorothy Widenmann Foundation

Fig. 30

Nahua noblewoman preparing chocolate drink. Codex Tudela, 16th century pictorial Aztec codex. Museum of the Americas, Madrid, Spain.

Heritage Pics/Alamy Stock Images

Fig. 31

Santa Maria de Jesus, Guatemala - August 20, 2017: Colorful Sunday market in front of church in small indigenous town on slopes of Agua volcano near UNESCO World Heritage Site of Antigua. Istock.

CHAPTER 5

Fig. 32

Codex Zouche-Nuttall

Marriage Lord Eight Deer, Mixtec, A.D. 1350

Met Museum, New York

Fig. 33

Archeological site of Monte Albán (500 BC-AD 1000). "Danzantes". UNESCO World Heritage Site. Oaxaca, Mexico.

Alamy Stock Photo

Fig. 34

Zelia Nuttall

The History Collection/ Alamy Stock Photo

Fig. 35

Façade of the Peabody Museum of Archaeology and Ethnology, Harvard University, Boston, USA.

Neilann Tait/Alamy Stock Photo

Fig. 36

The Codex Zouche-Nuttall is an accordion-folded pre-Columbian 14th century, document of Mixtec pictography, now in the collection of the British Museum.

World History Archive/Alamy Stock Photo

CHAPTER 6

Fig. 37

The Great City of Tenochtitlan, Diego Rivera (1886-1957). Palacio Nacional, Mexico City, Mexico.

Bridgeman Images

Fig. 38

Florentine Codex Fol. 1 Mercaderes de plumas, ropa, metates.

Art Collection 3/Alamy

Fig. 39

Florentine Codex. Pochteca. The Picture Art Collection. Alamy Stock Photo

Fig. 40

Florentine Codex, Folio IX Vendors of textiles, food goods, chairs, turkeys.

The Picture Art Collection/Alamy Stock Photo

Fig. 41

"The Market of Tlatelolco." Diego Rivera (1866-1957). Palacio Nacional, Mexico City, Mexico.

Bridgeman Images

CHAPTER 7

Fig. 42

Malinche (c. 1496-1529) Nahual woman. Interpreter of the Spanish conqueror Hernán Cortes. Mexican Engraving, 1885. Colored.

Prisma Archivo/Alamy Stock Photo

Fig. 43

Tecoaccinco. History of Tlaxcala by Diego Munoz Camargo, 1585.

WHPics/Alamy Stock Photo

Fig. 44

Cortes arrived at the Tlaxcalan town of Xaltelolco. Plate 27 of History of Tlaxcala by Diego Munoz Camargo. HeritagePics/Alamy Stock Photo

Fig. 45

The Storming of Teocalli by Cortes and his Troops. Emanuel Leutze, 1848. Oil on canvas.

Wadsworth Athenaeum, Hartford, Connecticut.

Fig. 46

Battle for the fortress of Xoloc. Plate 45 of History of Tlaxcala by Diego Munoz Camargo, 1585.

HeritagePics/Alamy Stock Photo

Fig. 47

Fray Bartolome de las Casas (1474-1566). Heritage Image Partnership/Alamy Stock Photo

Fig. 48

Cocos or cacao bean, Theobroma cacao, with section through fruit showing seeds. Handcoloured stipple copperplate engraving by Lambert Junior from a drawing by Pierre Jean-Francois Turpin from Chameton, Poiret et Chamberet's "La Flore Medicale," Paris, Panckoucke, 1830. Pierre Joseph Redoute and Pancrace Bessa.

Album/Alamy Stock Photo

CHAPTER 8

Fig. 49

Antique illustration of scene of daily life in a convent. Istock

Fig. 50

Diego de Valades (1533-1582). The Great Chain of Being from his 1579 Rhetorica Christiana.

Pictoral Press Ltd./Alamy Stock Photo

Fig. 51

Vintage engraving of New testament, The Holy Women, 19th Century. James Tissot.
Istock

CHAPTER 9

Fig. 52

Sor Juana Inés de la Cruz. Museo de América, Madrid, Spain. Bridgeman Images.

Fig. 53

Bernadette Soubirous caring for sick people 1877. Hi-Story/Alamy Stock Photo

Fig. 54

The Nuns at the Convent of Santa Maria Luton. Trinity Mirror/Mirrorpix/Alamy Stock Photo

CHAPTER 10

Fig. 55

Andres de Islas. Oil on canvas, *casta* painting, Mestizo. Viceroyalty of New Spain. Museum of the Americas. Madrid, Spain. PRISMA ARCHIVO/Alamy Stock Photo

Fig. 56

Witches burnt at the stake. Private Collection Archives Charmet/ Bridgeman Images

CHAPTER 11

Fig. 57

Elizabeth Fry speaking to the prisoners on a convict ship. Lithograph. The Stapleton Collection/ Bridgeman Images

Fig. 58

Napoleon on the morning of the Battle of Austerlitz, 1805. French School. Bridgeman Images.

Fig. 59

Chocolate: Spanish women at church. Chocolate served. Stefano Blanchetti/Bridgeman Images.

CHAPTER 12

Fig. 60

Ann of Austria (1601-1666) . Alamy Stock Photo

Fig. 61

Saint-Jean-Baptiste Church, St. Jean de Luz, France. Tuul and Bruno Morandi/ Alamy Stock Photo

Fig. 62

Marie Thérèse, portrait of the *infanta* of Spain. Lebrecht Music & Arts/Alamy Stock Photo

Fig. 63

Madame de Sévigné. 17th Century, Paris. Carnavalet Museum. The Artchives/Alamy Stock Photo

CHAPER 13

Fig. 64

Aerial view of Modica old town with San Pietro Cathedral, Sicily, Italy. Istock

Fig. 65

Eleonora di Toledo con figlio Giovanni. Archiviart/Alamy Stock Photo

Fig. 66

Vintage engraving of people Gathering Cinchona bark, Ecuador, 19th Century. Jesuit's Bark, also known as cinchona bark, as Peruvian Bark, and as China Bark, is a former name of the most celebrated specific remedy for all forms of malaria. Istock

Fig. 67

Santa Maria Novella pharmacy. Florence, Italy. AGF Sri/Alamy Stock Photo

Fig. 68

La Infanta Catalina Micaela, 1577-1578. Painted by El Greco. Album/Alamy Stock Photo

CHAPTER 14

Fig. 69

York, England

Alamy Stock Photo

Fig. 70

The Merchant Adventurers Hall. Yorkshire, England. robertharding/Alamy Stock Photo

Fig. 71

The Retreat York, England

Alamy Stock Photo

CHAPTER 15

Fig. 72

Curacao. Early evening light warms the candy-colored buildings line the waterfront at this UNESCO World Heritage Site. Istock.

CHAPTER 16

Fig. 73

Green Dragon Tavern. Boston, Massachusetts AlanHaynes.com/Alamy Stock Photo

Fig. 74

Document; De Lucena, Abraham Haim; De Lucena, Rachel; New York, New York, United States; 1726 March 24

1726-03-24

Colenda Digital Repository, Penn Libraries

Fig. 75

The Adverts 250 Project.

CHAPTER 17

Fig. 76

Mascaron. Place de la Bourse, Bordeaux, France. Mark Dunn/Alamy Stock Photo

Fig. 77

Homage to Maitte Adélaide Modeste Testas one of the many African trafficked in the 19th century.

KMcV/Alamy Stock Photo.

Fig. 78

Quito School. The Mulatto Gentlemen of Esmeraldas. Painted by Andrés Sánchez Gallque. Museo de America, Madrid, Spain. Album/Alamy Stock Photo

CHAPTER 18

Fig. 79

Rowntree's advertisement about 1910. Pictorial Press Ltd./Alamy Stock Photo

Fig. 80

Rowntree's Chocolates. Infinity Images/Alamy Stock Photo

Fig. 81

Chocolate coating machine. The Whitman Candy Co, Philadelphia, Pennsylvania. 1917-1918. Imago History Collection/Alamy Stock Photo

Fig. 82

Casa Amatller in Barcelona Spain. Istock.

Fig. 83

Reverie design by Alphonse Mucha. Vintage Images/Alamy Stock Photo

Fig. 84

A postcard advertising Maillard's Exhibit of "Fine Chocolates & Cocoa" and "Celebrated Confections" in the Agriculture Building of the 1893 World's Fair in Chicago. In the pavilion are the chocolate statues of Columbus (left), Venus (center), and a partially visible Minerva. hhttps://worldsfairchicago1893.com/

CHAPTER 19

Fig. 85

Luisa Spagnoli (1877-1935) Perugia, Italy. ARCHIVIO/Alamy Stock Photo

Fig. 86

City's symbol, the griffin of Perugia over grand portal of Palazzo dei Priori, Perugia, Umbria, Italy.

Manfred Gottschalk/ Alamy Stock Photo

Fig. 87

Luisa Spagnoli. ARCHIVIO GBB/Alamy Stock Photo

Fig. 88

Baci brand by Luisa Spagnoli. ARCHIBO GBB/Alamy Stock Photo

CHAPTER 20

Fig. 89

Vintage photograph of the Basilica del Voto Nacional, Quito, Ecuador. Istock

Fig. 90

Antonio de Pereda (1611-1678). Still life with Ebony Chest. Magite Historic/Alamy Stock Photo

Fig. 91

The Family of the Duke of Penthièvre. "La Tasse de Chocolat" by Jean-Baptiste Charpentier, oil on canvas. Bridgeman Images.

Fig. 92

Luis Egidio Meléndez (1716-1780) Spanish. Still life with Chocolate Service.

Artepics /Alamy Stock Image.

ENDPAGES

Cocos or cacao bean, Theobroma cacao, with section through fruit showing seeds. Handcoloured stipple copperplate engraving by Lambert Junior from a drawing by Pierre Jean-Francois Turpin from Chameton, Poiret et Chamberet's "La Flore Medicale," Paris, Panckoucke, 1830. Pierre Joseph Redoute and Pancrace Bessa.

Album/Alamy Stock Photo

Plant and butterfly from Metamorphosis insectorum Surinamensium (Surinam insects) a hand coloured 18th century Book by Maria Sibyllus Merian published in Amsterdam in 1719.

PhotoStock-Israel/Alamy Stock Photo

COVER

Nahua noblewoman preparing chocolate drink. Codex Tudela, 16th century pictorial Aztec codex. Museum of the Americas, Madrid, Spain.

Heritage Pics/Alamy Stock Images

Service personnel historical. SZ Photo/Scherl/Bridgeman Images.

DEDICATION PAGE

Suchard Chocolate, 19th century advertisement

Photo 12/Alamy Stock Photo

Bibliography

Aiton, Arthur S., and J. Lloyd Mecham. "The Archivo General De Indias." *The Hispanic American Historical Review* 4, no. 3 (1921): 553–67. https://doi.org/10.2307/2506057.

"Aztec Picture Writing: The Story of the 'Codex Nutalli.'" *The New Era Lancaster* (Lancaster, PA). March 26, 1902. Accessed December 16, 2021. Newspapers.com.

Baci Perugina. "Facts and Figures." N.d. Accessed July 27, 2021. https://www.baciperugina.com/intl/world/blog/news/facts-and-figures.

Baci Perugina. "I Love Love Notes." October 17, 2018. https://www.baciperugina.com/intl/world/blog/news/love-notes.

Balch, Oliver. "Mars, Nestlé and Hershey to Face Child Slavery Lawsuit in US." *The Guardian*. February 12, 2021. https://www.theguardian.com/global-development/2021/feb/12/mars-nestle-and-hershey-to-face-landmark-child-slavery-lawsuit-in-us.

Behar, Ruth. "Sex and Sin, Witchcraft and the Devil in Late-Colonial Mexico." *American Ethnologist* 14, no. 1 (1987): 34–54. http://www.jstor.org/stable/645632.

Berdan, Frances F. "Aztec Merchants and Markets: Local-Level Economic Activity in a Non-Industrial Empire." *Mexicon* 2, no. 3 (1980): 37–41. http://www.jstor.org/stable/23757459.

"Personal." *Boston Evening Transcript*. August 16, 1892. Accessed December 16, 2021. https://www.newspapers.com/image/735190977/?terms=Boston%20Evening%20Transcript%20Nuttall&match=1.

Cabezon, Beatriz, and Louis Evan Grivetti. "Symbols from Ancient Times: Paleography and the St. Augustine Chocolate Saga." In *Chocolate: History, and Heritage*, edited by Louis Evan Grivetti and Howard-Yana Shapiro, 669–98. Davis, CA: John Wiley and Sons, 2009.

Cabezon, Beatriz, Patricia Barriga, and Louis E. Grivetti, "Chocolate and Sinful Behaviors." In *Chocolate: History, Culture, and Heritage*, edited by Louis E. Grivetti and Howard-Yana Shapiro, 37–48. Davis, CA: John Wiley & Sons, 2009.

Carletti, Francesco. *My Voyage Around the World: The Chronicles of a 16th Century Florentine Merchant.* Translated by Herbert Weinstock. New York: Pantheon Books, 1964.

Cervantes, Gabriel. "Convict Transportation and Penitence in 'Moll Flanders.'" *ELH* 78, no. 2 (2011): 315–36. http://www.jstor.org/stable/41236546.

Chocolate Class. "Chocolate-Coated Sacrifices: A History of Cacao and Blood in Mesoamerica." March 25, 2020. https://chocolateclass.wordpress.com/2020/03/25/chocolate-coated-sacrifices-a-history-of-cacao-and-blood-in-mesoamerica/

Chocolate Class. "How Women Are Portrayed in Chocolate Advertising." April 8, 2016. https://chocolateclass.wordpress.com/2016/04/08/how-women-are-portrayed-in-chocolate-advertising/.

Chocolate Class. "Naughty but Nice: Gendered Sexualization in Chocolate Advertising." May 14, 2017. https://chocolateclass.wordpress.com/2017/05/14/naughty-but-nice-gendered-sexualization-in-chocolate-advertising/.

"Chocolate Companies Face New Charges of Child Slavery." Freedom United, February 19, 2001. https://www.freedomunited.org/news/chocolate-companies-face-new-charges/.

"Chocolate and Feminism: Exploring the Changing Role of Women in Rowntree's Chocolate and Cocoa Advertisements, 1930–1960." *The York Historian*, November 7, 2017. https://theyorkhistorian.com/2017/11/07/chocolate-and-feminism-exploring-the-changing-role-of-women-in-rowntrees-chocolate-and-cocoa-advertisements-1930-1960/.

Chrystal, Paul, and Joe Dickinson. *History of Chocolate in York.* Pen & Sword Books. Kindle.

CIRAD. "The Indians of the Ecuadorian Amazon Were Using Cocoa 5,300 Years Ago." October 30, 2018. https://www.eurekalert.org/pub_releases/2018-10/c-tio103018.php.

Coe, Sophie D., and Michael D. Coe. *The True History of Chocolate.* London: Thames & Hudson, 2013.

"De Lucena, Abraham Haim; De Lucena, Rachel; New York, New York, United States; 1726 March 24." Arnold and Deanne Kaplan Collection of Early American Judaica. Colenda Digital Repository. University of Pennsylvania, Philadelphia. https://colenda.library.upenn.edu/catalog/81431-p38s4jt9n.

Córdoba Toro, Julián. "Catalina Bustamante La Primera Maestra de América." *Iberoamérica Social*, July 30, 2020. https://iberoamericasocial.com/catalina-bustamante-la-primera-maestra-de-america/.

Cummins, Tom. "Three Gentlemen from Esmeraldas: A Portrait Fir for a King." In *Slave Portraiture in the Atlantic World*, edited by Agnes Lugo-Ortiz and Angela Rosenthal, 119–45. New York: Cambridge University Press, 2013.

"Cymbopetalum penduliflorum Orejuela Ear Flower." *Reports by FLAAR Mesoamerica on Flora & Fauna of Parque Nacional Yaxha Nakum Naranjo Peten, Guatemala, Central America*, March 11, 2013. http://www.maya-ethnobotany.org/images-mayan-ethnobotanicals-medicinal-plants-tropical-agriculture-flower-spice-flavoring/cymbopetalum-penduliflorum-orejuela-ear-flower-images.php.

D'Souza, Romana. "Why Women Should East Chocolate." *India Times*. Updated June 25, 2014. https://www.indiatimes.com/health/healthyliving/why-women-should-eat-more-chocolate-242166.html.

Day, Ivan, and Peter Brown. *Pleasures at the Table: Ritual and Display in the European Dining Room, 1600–1900*. York, UK: York Civic Trust, 1997.

Dewan, Leslie, and Dorothy Hosler. "Ancient Maritime Trade on Balsa Rafts: An Engineering Analysis." *Journal of Anthropological Research* 64, no. 1 (2008): 19–40. http://www.jstor.org/stable/20371179.

Díaz del Castillo, Bernal. *The True History of the Conquest of New Spain: The Memoirs of the Conquistador Bernal Diaz del Castillo*, unabridged ed., vols. 1–2. York, UK: FV Editions, 2020.

Dibble, Charles E., and Arthur J. O. Anderson. *Florentine Codes: General History of the Things of New Spain: The Merchants, Fray Bernardino de Sahagún*. Santa Fe, NM: The School of American Research and The University of Utah, 1959.

Dreiss, Meredith L., and Sharon E. Greenhill. *Chocolate Pathway to the Gods*. Tucson: The University of Arizona Press, 2008.

Dunn, Patrick D. "The Oldest True Stories in the World." *Anthropology Magazine*, October 2018. https://www.sapiens.org/language/oral-tradition/.

Dupuy, Alex. "French Merchant Capital and Slavery in Saint-Domingue." *Latin American Perspectives* 12, no. 3 (1985): 77–102. http://www.jstor.org/stable/2633905.

"Ecuador's Chocolate Secret Is a Sustainable Reality." Global Newswire, January 6, 2010. Accessed June 30, 2021. https://www.globenewswire.com/en/news-release/2010/01/06/1254248/0/en/Ecuador-s-Chocolate-Secret-Is-a-Sustainable-Reality.html.

Estes, J. Worth. "The European Reception of the First Drugs from the New World." *Pharmacy in History* 37, no. 1 (1995): 3–23. http://www.jstor.org/stable/41111660.

Few, Martha. "Chocolate, Sex, and Disorderly Women in Late-Seventeenth and Early-Eighteenth-Century Guatemala." *Ethnohistory* 52, no. 4 (October 2005): 673–87. https://doi.org/10.1215/00141801-52-4-673

"Forgotten Territories, Unrealized Rights: Rural Afro-Ecuadorians and their Fight for Land, Equality, and Security A Report from the Rapoport Delegation on Afro-Ecuadorian Land Rights November 2009." The Bernard and Audre Rapoport Center for Human Rights and Justice, the University of Texas at Austin School of Law, November 2009. Accessed July 2, 2021. https://law.utexas.edu/wp-content/uploads/sites/31/2016/02/ecuador-eng.pdf.

Fraser, Antonia. *Love and Louis XIV: The Women in the Life of the Sun King*. New York: Anchor Books, 2006.

Gay, James F. "Chocolate Makers in 18th Century Pennsylvania." In *Chocolate: History, Culture, and Heritage*, edited by Louis Evan Grivetti and Howard-Yana Shapiro, 389–98. Davis, CA: Wiley and Sons, 2009.

Gay, James F. "Chocolate Production and Uses in 17th and 18th Century North America." In *Chocolate: History, Culture, and Heritage*, edited by Louis Evan Grivetti and Howard-Yana Shapiro, 281–300. Davis, CA: John Wiley and Sons, 2009.

Gelfand, Noah L. "The Gomez Family and Atlantic Patterns in the Development of New York's Jewish Community." The Gotham Center for New York History, July 21, 2020. https://www.gothamcenter.org/blog/the-gomez-family-and-atlantic-patterns-in-the-development-of-new-yorks-jewish-community.

George Washington's Mount Vernon. "The Washingtons and Chocolate." N.d. Accessed July 25, 2021. https://www.mountvernon.org/inn/recipes/the-washingtons-and-chocolate/.

Goldsmith, Lewis. *Memoir of the Court of St. Cloud: Being Secret Letters from a Gentleman at Paris to a Nobleman in London*. Boston: L. C. Page and Company, 1900. https://www.gutenberg.org/files/3899/3899-h/3899-h.htm

Grivetti, Louis E., and Howard-Yana Shapiro. *Chocolate: History, Culture, and Heritage*: Hoboken, NJ: John Wiley & Sons, 2009.

Grivetti, Louis Evan. "Chocolate Crime, and the Courts: Selected English Trial Documents, 1693–1834," In *Chocolate History, Culture, and Heritage*, edited by Louis Evan Grivetti and Howard-Yana Shapiro, 234–54. Davis, CA; John Wiley & Sons, 2009.

Gunnars, Kris. "7 Proven Health Benefits of Dark Chocolate." *Healthline*. N.d. Last reviewed July 27, 2021. Accessed June 15, 2021. https://www.healthline.com/nutrition/7-health-benefits-dark-chocolate#TOC_TITLE_HDR_5.

Hales, Dianne. "Italy's Passionate Women: The Chocolate Maker Who Created 'Baci.'" March 10, 2020. https://diannehales.com/italys-passionate-women-the-chocolate-maker-who-created-baci/.

Haring, C. C. "The Early Spanish Colonial Exchequer." *The American Historical Review* 23, no. 4 (July 1918): 779–96. https://doi.org/10.1086/ahr/23.4.779.

Haskell, Yasmin. "Poetry or Pathology? Jesuit Hypochondria in Early Modern Naples." *Early Science and Medicine* 12, no. 2 (2007): 187–213. http://www.jstor.org/stable/20617663.

Helland, Janice. "Aztec Imagery in Frida Kahlo's Paintings: Indigenity and Political Commitment." *Woman's Art Journal* 11, no. 2 (1990): 8–13. http://www.jstor.org/stable/3690692.

Hembree, Mikelle. "Buying Sweets from Nuns in Seville-Dulces de Conventos." *City Nibbler, Nibbling My Way Through One City at a Time*, May 14, 2018. https://www.citynibbler.com/home/2018/5/14/buying-sweets-from-nuns-in-seville-dulces-de-conventos.

Henderson, Paul. "Cocoa, Finance and the State in Ecuador, 1895–1925." *Bulletin of Latin American Research* 16, no. 2 (1997): 169–86. http://www.jstor.org/stable/3339105.

Hershkowitz, Leo. "Original Inventories of Early New York Jews (1682–1763) (Concluded)." *American Jewish History* 90, no. 4 (2002): 385–448. http://www.jstor.org/stable/23887216.

Hilton, Phil. "The Secrets behind Advertising Chocolate to Women and Why It's about to Change Forever." *Stylist*, 2015. https://www.stylist.co.uk/life/do-chocolate-firms-target-women-flake-cadburys-sweets-confectionery/58560.

Hirth, Kenneth G. *The Aztec Economic World: Merchants and Markets in Ancient Mesoamerica.* New York: Cambridge University Press, 2016.

Huici Miranda, Ambrosio. *La cocina hispano-magrebí durante la época almohade.* Gijón, Spain: Ediciones Trea, S.L., 2016.

The International Association of Research Institutes in the History of Art. "Instituto Amatller de Arte Hispánico." N.d. Accessed July 9, 2021. http://www.riha-institutes.org/Institutes/IAAH.

Jewish Virtual Library. "Lucena, Spain." N.d. Accessed May 11, 2021. https://www.jewishvirtuallibrary.org/lucena-spain-virtual-jewish-history-tour

Jewish Virtual Library. "Modern Jewish History: The Jewish Expulsion 1492." N.d. Accessed May 11, 2021. https://www.jewishvirtuallibrary.org/the-spanish-expulsion-1492.

Johns Hopkins Medicine. "The Benefits of Having a Healthy Relationship with Chocolate." N.d. Accessed July 25, 2021. https://www.hopkinsmedicine.org/health/wellness-and-prevention/the-benefits-of-having-a-healthy-relationship-with-chocolate.

Jones, Kenneth. "Review of Sangre de Drago (*Croton lechleri*)—A South American Tree Sap in the Treatment of Diarrhea, Inflammation, Insect Bites, Viral Infections, and Wounds: Traditional Uses to Clinical Research." *Journal of Alternative Complementary Medicine* 9, no. 6 (2003): 877–96. https://pubmed.ncbi.nlm.nih.gov/14736360/

Joy of Museums Virtual Tours. "'The Kiss' by Francesco Hayez." N.d. Accessed July 27, 2021. https://joyofmuseums.com/museums/europe/italy-museums/milan-museums/brera-art-gallery-pinacoteca-di-brera/the-kiss-by-francesco-hayez/.

Joyce, Arthur A., Andrew G. Workinger, Byron Hamann, Peter Kroefges, Maxine Oland, and Stacie M. King. "Lord 8 Deer 'Jaguar Claw' and the Land of the Sky: The Archaeology and History of Tututepec." *Latin American Antiquity* 15, no. 3 (2004): 273–97. https://doi.org/10.2307/4141575.

Kerr, Barbara, and Justin Kerr. "The 'Way' of God L: The Princeton Vase Revisited." *Record of the Art Museum, Princeton University* 64 (2005): 71–79. http://www.jstor.org/stable/3774836.

Keyes, Carl Robert. "Jonathan Crathorne." Adverts 250 Project, February 14, 2018. https://adverts250project.org/tag/jonathan-crathorne/.

Kurtz, Donald V. "Peripheral and Transitional Markets: The Aztec Case." *American Ethnologist* 1, no. 4 (1974): 685–705. http://www.jstor.org/stable/643375.

Lange, Amanda. "Baby It's Cold Outside: A Sweet History of Chocolate in New England." *Historic Deerfield*, n.d. Accessed July 23, 2021. https://www.historic-deerfield.org/blog/2021/1/4/baby-its-cold-outside-a-sweet-history-of-chocolate-in-new-england.

Lathrap, Donald W. "The Antiquity and Importance of Long-Distance Trade Relationships in the Moist Tropics of Pre-Columbian South America." *World Archaeology* 5, no. 2 (1973): 170–86. http://www.jstor.org/stable/123986.

Lavrin, Asunción. *Brides of Christ: Conventual Life in Colonial Mexico*. Stanford, CA: Stanford University Press, 2008.

Le Nouvelliste. "Lorraine Manuel Steed, digne héritiére de Modesta Testas." June 5, 2019. Accessed July 31, 2021. https://lenouvelliste.com/article/202730/lorraine-manuel-steed-digne-heritiere-de-modeste-testas.

Lippi, Donatella. "Chocolate in History: Food, Medicine, Medi-Food." *Nutrients* 5, no. 5 (2013): 1573–84. https://doi.org/10.3390/nu5051573

MacKay, Kathryn L. "The Chocolate Dippers' Strike of 1910." *Utah Historical Quarterly* 83, no. 1 (2015): 38–51. https://issuu.com/utah10/docs/uhq_volume83_2015_number1/s/10121983.

Macpherson, Catherine. "Chocolate's Early History in Canada." In *Chocolate: History, Culture, and Heritage*, edited by Louis Evan Grivetti and Howard-Yana Shapiro, 300–28. Davis, CA: John Wiley and Sons, 2009.

Mallon, Edward. A. "Cinchona Bark and Louis XIV." *JAMA* 171, no. 14 (1959): 1990. https://jamanetwork.com/journals/jama/article-abstract/327211

Marcus, Joyce. "A Comparison of the Zapotec and Maya." *World Archaeology* 10, no. 2 (October 1978):172–91. https://doi.org/10.1080/00438243.1978.9979729.

McNeill, Leila. "The Archaeologist who Helped Mexico Find Glory in Its Indigenous Past." *Smithsonian Magazine*, November 5, 2018. https://www.smithsonianmag.com/science-nature/archaeologist-who-helped-mexico-find-glory-its-past-180970700/.

Miller, Mary, and Karl Taube. *An Illustrated Dictionary of The Gods and Symbols of Ancient Mexico and the Maya*. London: Thames & Hudson, 2014.

Molleda Castillo, Rosa Ernestina. "Delicias de antaño. Historia y recetas de los conventos Mexicanos: Convento de Santa Clara, 1570. Convento de San Jerónimo, 1585. El dulce en México,sus dulces, confituras y ambrosias." *Culinary Art School*. http://www.culinaryartschool.edu.mx/cocinasdemexico/wp-content/uploads/2016/07/Bloque-20-Actividad-1-Unidad-4.pdf.

Moncorgé, Marie Josèph. *Medieval Cookbooks in Andalusia*. Translated by Carl Crosby. N.d. Accessed March 24, 2021. https://www.oldcook.com/en/medieval-cookery_books_andalusia

Monello, Paolo. *Anna Cabrera E Federico Enriquez Conti di Modica (1480–1538)*. Palermo: Edizione Ridotta, 2012.

Mucha Foundation. "Advertising Posters." N.d. Accessed July 9, 2021. http://www.muchafoundation.org/en/gallery/themes/theme/advertising-posters/object/42.

Nag, Oishimaya Sen. "Which Countries Eat the Most Chocolate." *World Atlas*. September 27, 2018. https://www.worldatlas.com/articles/which-countries-eat-the-most-chocolate.html

The National WWI Museum and Memorial. "Italy Enters World War I." N.d. Accessed July 27, 2021. www.theworldwar.org/learn/wwi/italy.

NBC News. "Once on Display, This Shrunken Head Is Returning to the Amazon." May 11, 2021. https://www.nbcnews.com/science/science-news/display-ceremonial-head-returning-amazon-rcna884.

Newson, Linda A. "Medical Practice in Early Colonial Spanish America: A Prospectus." *Bulletin of Latin American Research* 25, no. 3 (2006): 367–91. http://www.jstor.org/stable/27733871

Norton, Marcy. "Conquests of Chocolate." *OAH Magazine of History* 18, no. 3 (2004): 14–17. http://www.jstor.org/stable/25163677.

Norton, Marcy. "Conquests of Chocolate." *OAH Magazine of History* 18, no. 3 (April 2004): 14–17. https://doi.org/10.1093/maghis/18.3.14.

Norton, Marcy. "Tasting Empire: Chocolate and the European Internalization of Mesoamerican Aesthetics." *The American Historical Review* 111, no. 3 (2006): 660–91. https://doi.org/10.1086/ahr.111.3.660.

Norton, Marcy. "Tasting Empire: Chocolate and the European Internationalization of Mesoamerican Aesthetics." *The American Historical Review* 111, no. 3 (June 2006): 660–91. https://doi.org/10.1086/ahr.111.3.660

Norton, Marcy. *Sacred Gifts, Profane Pleasures. A History of Tobacco and Chocolate in the Atlantic World.* Ithaca, NY: Cornell University Press, 2008.

Nuttall, Zelia. "Ancient Mexican Superstitions." *Journal of American Folklore* 10, no. 39 (October–December 1897): 265–81. https://doi.org/10.2307/233278.

Off, Carol. *Bitter Chocolate: Anatomy of an Industry.* New York: Random House, 2006.

Olko, Justyna, and Agnieszka Brylak. "Defending Local Autonomy and Facing Cultural Trauma: A Nahua Order against Idolatry, Tlaxcala, 1543." *Hispanic American Historical Review* 98, no. 4 (2018): 573–604. https://www.academia.edu/38041538/Defending_Local_Autonomy_and_Facing_Cultural_Trauma_A_Nahua_Order_against_Idolatry_Tlaxcala_1543.

Patrimonio Cultural. "Casa Amatller: The Façade of Chocolate." N.d. Accessed July 9, 2021. http://patrimoni.gencat.cat/en/collection/casa-amatller

Pecorelli, Sabrina. "The Hidden Ingredient in Chocolate: Africa's Child Slaves." *Charged Affairs. YPFP's Foreign Policy Journal*, April 27, 2020. https://chargedaffairs.org/.

Pérez, Joseph. *The Spanish Inquisition.* New Haven, CT, and London: Yale University Press, 2005.

"The Pinart-Nuttall Wedding." *San Francisco Chronicle.* May 11, 1880. Accessed July 9, 2021. Newspapers.com.

Plouvier, Liliane. *L'Europe se met à Table.* Brussels: Commission européene et le Parlement européene, 2000. https://www.oldcook.com/doc/plouvier_europe_table.pdf

Pound, Cath. "How Alphonse Mucha's Iconic Posters Came to Define Art Nouveau." *Artsy.net*, November 13, 2018. Accessed July 9, 2021. https://www.artsy.net/article/artsy-editorial-alphonse-muchas-iconic-posters-define-art-nouveau.

Presilla, Maricel E. *The New Taste of Chocolate*. Berkeley, CA: Ten Speed Press, 2009.

The Princeton Vase A.D. 570–750. Princeton University Art Museum. https://artmuseum.princeton.edu/collections/objects/32221bid.

Prinz, D. "A Jewish Matriarch of American Chocolate Making." *On the Chocolate Trail*, May 5, 2013. Accessed July 25, 2021. https://onthechocolatetrail.org/2013/05/a-jewish-matriarch-of-american-chocolate-making/.

Quakers in the World. "The Retreat, York, England." N.d. Accessed July 19, 2021. https://www.quakersintheworld.org/quakers-in-action/92/The-Retreat-York-England.

Rabbi Prinz, Deborah. *On the Chocolate Trail*. Woodstock, VT: Jewish Lights Publishing, 2015.

Robertson, Emma. *Chocolate, Women, and Empire: A Social and Cultural History*. Manchester, UK: Manchester University Press, 2009.

Sévigné, Marie. *Madame de Sévigné: Selected Letters*. London: Penguin Classics, 1982.

Shapiro, Celia. "Nation of Nowhere." In *Chocolate: History, Culture and Heritage*, edited by Louis Evan Grivetti and Howard-Yana Shapiro, 49–65. Davis, CA: John Wiley and Sons, 2009.

Smith, Michael E. "The Aztec Marketing System and Settlement Pattern in the Valley of Mexico: A Central Place Analysis." *American Antiquity* 44, no. 1 (1979): 110–25. https://doi.org/10.2307/279193.

Sousa, Lis. *The Woman Who Turned into a Jaguar and Other Narratives of Native Women in Archives of Colonial Mexico*. Stanford, CA: Stanford University Press, 2017.

Strevens, Summer. "Mary Tuke: The Mother of York's Chocolate Industry." *On: Yorkshire Magazine*, n.d. Accessed March 24, 2021. https://www.on-magazine.co.uk/yorkshire/history/mary-tuke-york-chocolate-industry/.

Strocchia, Sharon T. "The Nun Apothecaries of Renaissance Florence: Marketing Medicines in the Convent." *Renaissance Studies* 25, no. 5 (2011): 627–47. http://www.jstor.org/stable/24420278.

Sturma, Michael. "Eye of the Beholder: The Stereotype of Women Convicts, 1788–1852." *Labour History*, no. 34 (1978): 3–10. https://doi.org/10.2307/27508305.

Thomas Jefferson Foundation. "Extract from Thomas Jefferson to John Adams." N.d. Accessed July 25, 2021. https://tjrs.monticello.org/letter/1789.

To Issue Valuable Volume. *Berkeley Daily Gazette* (Berkeley, CA). May 5, 1904. Newspapers.com

Townsend, Camilla. *Malintzin's Choices*. Albuquerque: University of New Mexico Press, 2006.

Tuke Family Collection 1660–1946. Borthwick Institute for Archives, University of York, England. Accessed July 18, 2021. https://borthcat.york.ac.uk/index.php/tuke.

UNESCO. "French Slave Trade." *Slavery and Remembrance*, n.d. Accessed July 1, 2021. http://slaveryandremembrance.org/articles/article/?id=A0097

UNESCO. "Mayo Chinchipe-Marañon Archaeological Landscape." World Heritage Convention, n.d. Accessed July 9, 2021. https://whc.unesco.org/en/tentativelists/6091/.

University of British Columbia, Open Case Studies. "Why the Struggles of the Shuar Indigenous People in Ecuador Conserve Their Culture Are Key to Local Conservation." N.d. Accessed March 24, 2021. https://cases.open.ubc.ca/why-the-struggles-of-the-shuar-indigenous-people-in-ecuador-to-conserve-their-culture-are-key-to-local-conservation/

Valdez, Francisco. "Early Complexity in the Upper Amazon: The Mayo Chinchipe-Marañón." Presentation at the 81st Annual Meeting of the Society for American Archaeology, Orlando, Florida, 2016 (tDAR id: 402955).

Vargas-Betancourt, Margarita. "Pochtecas, productoras y vendedoras: mujeres tlatelolcas en la ciudad de México durante el siglo XVI." In *Los Oficios en las sociedades indianas*, edited by Felipe Castro Gutiérrez and Isabel M. Povea Moreno, 71–100. México City: Universidad Nacional Autónoma de México, Instituto de Investigaciones Historícas, 2020.

Vistas Gallery. "The Mulatto Gentleman of Esmeraldas." 2015. Accessed July 1, 2021. https://vistasgallery.ace.fordham.edu/items/show/1903.

Walt, Vivienne. "Big Chocolate Wins Its Child-Labor Case in Supreme Court." *Fortune Magazine*, June 17, 2021. https://fortune.com/2021/06/17/child-labor-case-supreme-court-big-chocolate-nestle-cargill-scotus/.

Ward, Gerald. "Silver Chocolate Pots of Colonial Boston." In *Chocolate: History, Culture and Heritage*, edited by Louis Evan Grivetti and Howard-Yana Shapiro, 143–56. Davis, CA: John Wiley and Sons, 2009.

Waterson, Luke. "Spilling the Beans: Exploring Ecuador's Elusive Chocolate Industry." *Lonely Planet*, December 13, 2015. Accessed July 22, 2021. https://www.lonelyplanet.com/articles/spilling-the-beans-exploring-ecuadors-elusive-chocolate-industry.

Watson, Gwen. "Crazy Valentine Day's Facts." *Gourmet Gift Baskets*. February 3, 2021. https://www.gourmetgiftbaskets.com/Blog/post/crazy-valentines-day-facts.aspx.

Williams, Robert L. *The Complete Codex Zouche-Nuttall*. Austin: University of Texas Press, 2013.

Women of the Page: Convent Culture in the Early Modern Spanish World. Exhibition, Brown University, 2017. https://jcblibrary.org/exhibitions/women-page-convent-culture-early-modern-spanish-world

Zarrillo, Sonia, Nilesh Gaikwad, Claire Lanaud, Terry Powis, Christopher Viot, Isabelle Lesur, Olivier Fouet, Xavier Argout, Erwan Guichoux, Franck Salin, Rey Loor Solorzano, Olivier Bouchez, Hélène Vignes, Patrick Severts, Julio Hurtado, Alexandra Yepez, Louis Grivetti, Michael Blake, and Francisco Valdez. "The Use and Domestication of Theobroma Cacao during the Mid-Holocene in the Upper Amazon." *Nature Ecology & Evolution* 2 (2018): 1879–1888. https://doi.org/10.1038/s41559-018-0697-x.

Zorich, Zach. "Ancient Amazonian Chocolatiers." *Archaeology Magazine*, January/February 2019. https://www.archaeology.org/issues/325-1901/trenches/7219-trenches-ecuador-cacao-seeds.

Endnotes

1. Jewish Virtual Library. *Modern Jewish History: the Jewish Expulsion 1492*. https://www.jewishvirtuallibrary.org/the-spanish-expulsion-1492.

2. Sabrina Pecorelli. *The Hidden Ingredient in Chocolate: Africa's Child Slaves*. April 27, 2020. Charged Affairs. YPFP's Foreign Policy Journal. https://chargedaffairs.org/.

3. CIRAD, "The Indians of the Ecuadorian Amazon were using cocoa 5,300 years ago." (October 30, 2018)https://www.eurekalert.org/pub_releases/2018-10/c-tio103018.php.

4. Ibid.

5. Patrick D. Dunn. *The Oldest True Stories in the World*. Anthropology Magazine. October 2018. https://www.sapiens.org/language/oral-tradition/.

6. Francisco Valdez. *Early Complexity in the Upper Amazon: The Mayo Chinchipe-Marañón*. Presented at The 81st Annual Meeting of the Society for American Archaeology, Orlando, Florida. 2016 (tDAR id: 402955)

7. UNESCO. *Mayo Chinchipe-Marañon archaeological landscape*. World Heritage Convention. https://whc.unesco.org/en/tentativelists/6091/

8. NBC News. *Once on Display, This Shrunken Head is Returning to the Amazon*. May 11, 2021. https://www.nbcnews.com/science/science-news/display-ceremonial-head-returning-amazon-rcna884.

9. Ibid.

10. Sonia Zarrillo, Nilesh Gaikwad, Claire Lanaud, Terry Powis, Christopher Viot, Isabelle Lesur, OlivierFouet, Xavier Argout, Erwan Guichoux, Franck Salin, Rey Loor Solorzano, Olivier Bouchez, Hélène Vignes, Patrick Severts, Julio Hurtado, Alexandra Yepez, Louis Grivetti, Michael Blake, Francisco Valdez. **The use and domestication of Theobroma cacao during the mid-Holocene in the upper Amazon**. *Nature Ecology & Evolution*, 2018; DOI: 10.1038/s41559-018-0697-x

11. Ibid

12. https://whc.unesco.org/en/tentativelists/6091/

13. University of British Columbia, Open Cases, *Why the Struggles of the Shuar Indigenous People in Ecuador Conserve their Culture are key to local Conservation.* https://cases.open.ubc.ca/why-the-struggles-of-the-shuar-indigenous-people-in-ecuador-to-conserve-their-culture-are-key-to-local-conservation/

14. Zach Zorich. *Ancient Amazonian Chocolatiers.* Archaeology Magazine, Jan/Feb 2019. https://www.archaeology.org/issues/325-1901/trenches/7219-trenches-ecuador-cacao-seeds

15. Lathrap, Donald W. "The Antiquity and Importance of Long-Distance Trade Relationships in the Moist Tropics of Pre-Columbian South America." World Archaeology 5, no. 2 (1973): 170-86. Accessed June 3, 2021. http://www.jstor.org/stable/123986.

16. Ibid.

17. Dewan, Leslie, and Dorothy Hosler. "Ancient Maritime Trade on Balsa Rafts: An Engineering Analysis." Journal of Anthropological Research 64, no. 1 (2008): 19-40. Accessed May 31, 2021. http://www.jstor.org/stable/20371179.

18. Ibid.

19. Dreiss, Meredith L. Greenhill, Sharon E. *Chocolate Pathway to the Gods.* Tucson, Arizona: The University of Arizona Press, 2008.

20. Ibid, Page 58.

21. Ibid, Page 60.

22. Coe, Sophie D., Coe, Michael D. *The True History of Chocolate.* London, England: Thames & Hudson Ltd., 2013.

23. Ibid.

24. Ibid, Page 37.

25. Ibid, Page 37.

26. Grivetti, Louis E., Shapiro Howard-Yana. *Chocolate: History, Culture, and Heritage*: Hoboken, New Jersey: John Wiley & Sons, 2009.

27. Coe. Page 42.

28. Grivetti, Page 5.

29. Chocolate Class. *Chocolate-Coated Sacrifices: A History of Cacao and Blood in Mesoamerica, https://chocolateclass.wordpress.com/2020/03/25/chocolate-coated-sacrifices-a-history-of-cacao-and-blood-in-mesoamerica/*

30. The Princeton Vase A.D. 570-750. Princeton University art Museum. https://artmuseum.princeton.edu/collections/objects/32221bid

31. Ibid.

32. Kerr, Barbara, and Justin Kerr. "The "Way" of God L: The Princeton Vase Revisited." *Record of the Art Museum, Princeton University* 64 (2005): 71-79. Accessed June 9, 2021. http://www.jstor.org/stable/3774836.

33. Norton, Marcy. "Conquests of Chocolate." *OAH Magazine of History* 18, no. 3 (2004): 14-17. Accessed June 10, 2021. http://www.jstor.org/stable/25163677.

34. Reports by FLAAR Mesoamerica on Flora and Fauna of Parque Nacional Yaxha, Naku, Naranjo, Peten Guatemala Central America. Accessed June 14, 2021. www.Maya-Ethnobotany.org.

35. Marcus, Joyce. *A Comparison of the Zapotec and Maya.* World Archaeology. October 1978.

36. Sousa, Lis. *The Woman Who Turned into a Jaguar and other Narratives of Native Women in Archives of Colonial Mexico.* Stanford, California: Stanford University Press, 2017.

37. Ibid, Page 37.

38. Dreiss, Meredith L. Greenhill, Sharon Edgar. *Chocolate: Pathways to the Gods.* Tucson, Arizona: The University of Arizona Press, 2008.

39. Dibble Charles E., Anderson Arthur J.O., *Florentine Codes: General History of the Things of New Spain: The Merchants, Fray Bernardino de Sahagún.* Santa Fe, New Mexico: The School of American Research and The University of Utah, 1959

40. Coe. Page 93.

41. Ibid.

42. Joyce, Arthur A., Andrew G. Workinger, Byron Hamann, Peter Kroefges, Maxine Oland, and Stacie M. King. "Lord 8 Deer "Jaguar Claw" and the Land of the Sky: The Archaeology and History of Tututepec." *Latin American Antiquity* 15, no. 3 (2004): 273-97. Accessed June 15, 2021. doi:10.2307/4141575.

43. Williams Robert L. *The Complete Codex Zouche-Nuttall.* Austin, Texas: University of Texas Press, 2013.

44. Ibid. Page 285.

45. Miller, Mary, Taube, Karl. *An Illustrated Dictionary of The Gods and Symbols of Ancient Mexico and the Maya.* London, England: Thames & Hudson, 2014.

46. Nuttall, Zelia. "Ancient Mexican Superstitions" in *Journal of American Folklore.* Oct–Dec 1897 10:39, p. 266.

47. *The Pinart-Nuttall Wedding.* San Francisco Chronicle. Tuesday, May 11, 1880. Newspapers.com.

48. McNeill, Leila. "The Archaeologist who Helped Mexico Find Glory in Its Indigenous Past". Smithsonianmag.com, 5 November 2018.

49. McNeill.

50. *Boston Evening Transcript.* August 16, 1892. Newspapers.com.

51. Ibid.

52. *To Issue Valuable Volume. Berkeley Daily Gazette.* May 5, 1904. Newspapers.com

53. *The New Era Lancaster.* March 26, 1902. Newspapers.com

54. McNeill. Page 285.

55. McNeill, Page 4.

56. Ibid.

57. *The Feast of the Sun is Revived the Mexicans.*

58. Hirth, Kenneth G. *The Aztec Economic World: Merchants and Markets in Ancient Meso-america:* New York, New York, Cambridge University Press, 2016.

59. Ibid. Page 47.

60. Coe, Page 73.

61. Dreiss, Page 98.

62. Dibble, Page 39.

63. Ibid, Page 39.

64. Ibid, Page 29.

65. Hirth, Page 96.

66. Ibid, Page 204.

67. Ibid, Page 254.

68. Ibid, Page 121.

69. Ibid, Page 227.

70. Ibid, Page 47.

71. Ibid, Page 29.

72. Berdan, Frances F. "Aztec Merchants and Markets: Local-Level Economic Activity in a Non-Industrial Empire." *Mexicon* 2, no. 3 (1980): 37-41. Accessed June 18, 2021. http://www.jstor.org/stable/23757459.

73. Hirth. Page 17.

74. Smith, Michael E. "The Aztec Marketing System and Settlement Pattern in the Valley of Mexico: A Central Place Analysis." *American Antiquity* 44, no. 1 (1979): 110-25. Accessed June 18, 2021. doi:10.2307/279193.

75. Ibid. Page 111.

76. Ibid. Page 112.

77. Berdan. Page 2.

78. Kurtz, Donald V. "Peripheral and Transitional Markets: The Aztec Case." *American Ethnologist* 1, no. 4 (1974): 685-705. Accessed June 18, 2021. http://www.jstor.org/stable/643375.

79. Hirth, 186.

80. Kurtz. Page 694.

81. Ibid. Page 685.

82. Hirth, Page 322.

83. Ibid. Page 697.

84. Hirth, Page 209.

85. Coe. Page 99.

86. Ibid. 698.

87. Vargas-Betancourt, Margarita. "Pochtecas, productoras y vendedoras: mujeres tlatelol-cas en la ciudad de México durante el siglo XVI." Los Oficios en las sociedades indianas.

Felipe Castro Gutiérrez e Isabel M. Povea Moreno.Universidad Nacional Autónoma de México, Instituto de Investigaciones Historícas. 2020.

88. Díaz del Castillo, Bernal. *The True History of the Conquest of New Spain:The Memoirs of the Conquistador Bernal Diaz del Castillo,* Unabridged Edition Vol.1-2, 2020.

89. Hirth. Page 38.

90. Spores. Page 187.

91. Sousa. Page 206.

92. Ibid. Page 188.

93. Coe. Page 83.

94. Spores. Page 188.

95. Spores. Page 190.

96. Ibid.

97. Vargas-Bentancourt. Page 84.

98. Sousa, Page 185.

99. Sousa, Page 224.

100. People of the Townsend, Camilla. *Malintzin's Choices.* Albuquerque, New Mexico: University of New Mexico Press, 2006.

101. Ibid. Page 106.

102. Ibid. Page 133.

103. Ibid. Page 138.

104. Helland, Janice. "Aztec Imagery in Frida Kahlo's Paintings: Indigenity and Political Commitment." *Woman's Art Journal* 11, no. 2 (1990): 8-13. Accessed June 23, 2021. http://www.jstor.org/stable/3690692.

105. Coe. Page 109.

106. Ibid. Page 110.

107. Norton, Marcy . Conquests of Chocolate, *OAH Magazine of History,* Volume 18, Issue 3, April 2004, Pages 14–17, https://doi.org/10.1093/maghis/18.3.14

108. Haring, C.C. *The Early Spanish Colonial Exchequer:The American Historical Review,* Volume 23, Issue 4, July 1918.

109. Norton, Marcy. "Tasting Empire: Chocolate and the European Internalization of Mesoamerican Aesthetics." *The American Historical Review* 111, no. 3 (2006): 660-91. Accessed June 28, 2021. doi:10.1086/ahr.111.3.660. ges 779-796, https://doi.org/10.1086/ahr/23.4.779

110. Norton. Page 670.

111. Norton, Page 660.

112. Córdoba Toro, Julián. *Catalina Bustamante La Primera Maestra de América.* Iberoamérica Social. July 30, 2020. https://iberoamericasocial.com/catalina-bustamante-la-primera-maestra-de-america/

113. Olko, Justyna. Brylak, Agnieszka. *Defending Local Autonomy and Facing Cultural Trauma: A Nahua Order Against Idolatry, Tlaxcala, 1543*. Hispanic American Historical Review 98.4, 2018. https://www.academia.edu/38041538/Defending_Local_Autonomy_and_Facing_Cultural_Trauma_A_Nahua_Order_against_Idolatry_Tlaxcala_1543

114. Aiton, Arthur S., and J. Lloyd Mecham. "The Archivo General De Indias." *The Hispanic American Historical Review* 4, no. 3 (1921): 553-67. Accessed June 25, 2021. doi:10.2307/2506057.

115. Norton, Marcy. *Sacred Gifts, Profane Pleasures. A History of Tobacco and Chocolate in the Atlantic World*. Ithaca, New York: Cornell University Press, 2008.

116. Ibid . Page 147.

117. Ibid.

118. Norton. *Tasting Empire: Chocolate and the European Internationalization of Mesoamerican Aesthetics.*

119. Norton. *Sacred Gifts, Profane Pleasures.* Page 80.

120. Ibid. Page 78.

121. Ibid. Page 78.

122. Córdoba Toro.

123. Olko, Justyna. Brylak, Agnieszka. Page 588.

124. Córdoba.

125. Molleda Castillo, Rosa Ernestina. *Delicias de antaño. Historia y recetas de los conventos Mexicanos: Convento de Santa Clara, 1570. Convento de San Jerónimo, 1585. El dulce en México, sus dulces, confituras y ambrosias.* Culinary Art School. ernestinam@culinary-artschool.edu.mx.

126. Lavrin, Asunción. Brides of Christ: Conventual Life in Colonial Mexico. Stanford, CA: Stanford University Press, 2008.

127. Ibid. Page 151.

128. Lavrin. Page 22.

129. Tiffany, Tanya. Exhibition Curator. *Women of the Page: Convent Culture in the Early Modern Spanish World*. Providence, Rhode Island: Brown University, 2017. https://jcblibrary.org/exhibitions/women-page-convent-culture-early-modern-spanish-world

130. Ibid.

131. Plouvier, Liliane. *L'Europe se met à Table*. Brussels, Belgium: Commission européene et le Parlement européene. 2000. https://www.oldcook.com/doc/plouvier_europe_table.pdf

132. Ibid.

133. Newson, Linda A. "Medical Practice in Early Colonial Spanish America: A Prospectus." Bulletin of Latin American Research 25, no. 3 (2006): 367-91. Accessed July 2, 2021. http://www.jstor.org/stable/27733871.

134. Moncorgé. Marie Josèph. *Medieval Cookbooks in Andalusia. https://www.oldcook.com/en/medieval-cookery_books_andalusia*

135. Huici Miranda, Ambrosio. *La cocina hispano-magrebí durante la época almohade*. Gijón, Spain: Ediciones Trea, S.L., 2016.

136. Day, Ivan. Brown, Peter. *Pleasures at the Table.: Ritual and Display in the European Dining Room, 1600-1900*. York Civic Trust, 1997.

137. Norton, Marcy. "Tasting Empire: Chocolate and the European Internalization of Mesoamerican Aesthetics." The American Historical Review 111, no. 3 (2006): 660-91. Accessed July 3, 2021. doi:10.1086/ahr.111.3.660.

138. Hembree, Mikelle. *Buying Sweets from Nuns in Seville-Dulces de Conventos*. City Nibbler, Nibbling My Way Through One City at a Time. https://www.citynibbler.com/home/2018/5/14/buying-sweets-from-nuns-in-seville-dulces-de-conventos.

139. Few, Martha. Chocolate, Sex, and Disorderly Women in Late-Seventeenth and Early-Eighteenth-Century Guatemala. Ethnohistory 1 October 2005; 52 (4): 673–687. doi: https://doi.org/10.1215/00141801-52-4-673

140. Behar, Ruth. "Sex and Sin, Witchcraft and the Devil in Late-Colonial Mexico." *American Ethnologist* 14, no. 1 (1987): 34-54. Accessed July 3, 2021. http://www.jstor.org/stable/645632.

141. Ibid. Page 35.

142. Few. Page 675.

143. Ibid. Page 39.

144. Few. Page 674.

145. Beatriz Cabezon, Patricia Barriga, and Louis E. Grivetti, "Chocolate and Sinful Behaviors." Grivetti, Louis E., Shapiro, Howard-Yana. *Chocolate: History, Culture, and Heritage*. Davis, Ca: John Wiley & Sons, 2009.

146. Ibid. Page 40.

147. Few. Page 679.

148. Ibid. 680.

149. Ibid.

150. Grivetti, Louis Evan. Shapiro, Howard-Yana. *Chocolate: History, Culture, and Heritage*. Davis, CA: John Wiley & Sons, 2009.

151. Ibid. Page 44.

152. Pérez, Joseph. *The Spanish Inquisition*. New Haven and London; Yale University Press, 2005.

153. Ibid. Page 83.

154. Ibid.

155. Ibid. Page 252.

156. Grivetti, Louis Evan. "Chocolate Crime, and the Courts: Selected English Trial Documents, 1693-1834," Grivetti, Louis Evan. Shapiro, Howard-Yana. *Chocolate History, Culture, and Heritage*. Davis, Ca; John Wiley and Sons, 2009.

157. Ibid. Page 243.

158. CERVANTES, GABRIEL. "CONVICT TRANSPORTATION AND PENITENCE IN "MOLL FLANDERS"." *ELH* 78, no. 2 (2011): 315-36. Accessed July 6, 2021. http://www.jstor.org/stable/41236546.

159. Sturma, Michael. "Eye of the Beholder: The Stereotype of Women Convicts, 1788-1852." *Labour History*, no. 34 (1978): 3-10. Accessed July 6, 2021. doi:10.2307/27508305.

160. Goldsmith, Lewis. *Memoir of the Court of St. Cloud.* Project Gutenberg. https://www.gutenberg.org/files/3899/3899-h/3899-h.htm

161. Presilla, Maricel E. *The New Taste of Chocolate.* Berkeley; Ten Speed Press, 2009.

162. Fraser, Antonia. *Love and Louis XIV: The Women in the Life of the Sun King.* New York; Anchor Books, 2006.

163. Ibid. Page 85.

164. Fraser. Page 95.

165. Grivetti, Louis Evan. Shapiro, Howard-Yana. *Chocolate: History, Culture, and Heritage.* Davis; John Wiley & Sons, Inc.,2009.

166. Fraser. Page 86.

167. Grivetti. Page 571.

168. Fraser. Page 69.

169. Ibid. Page 87.

170. Fraser. Page 75.

171. Coe. Page 155.

172. Sévigné, Marie. *Madame de Sévigné: Selected Letters.* London; Penguin Classics, 1982.

173. Grivetti. Page 578.

174. Coe. Page 136.

175. Ibid.

176. Grivetti. Page 575.

177. Ibid. Page 577.

178. Haskell, Yasmin. "Poetry or Pathology? Jesuit Hypochondria in Early Modern Naples." *Early Science and Medicine* 12, no. 2 (2007): 187-213. Accessed July 13, 2021. http://www.jstor.org/stable/20617663.

179. Monello, Paolo. *Anna Cabrera E Federico Enriquez Conti di Modica (1480-1538)* Edizione Ridotta, 2012.

180. Grivetti. Page 260.

181. Lippi, Donatella. 2013. "Chocolate in History: Food, Medicine, Medi-Food" *Nutrients* 5, no. 5: 1573-1584. https://doi.org/10.3390/nu5051573

182. Ibid.

183. Ibid.

184. Ibid.

185. Carletti, Francesco. *My Voyage Around the World: The Chronicles of a 16th Century Florentine Merchant.* Translated from Italian by Herbert Weinstock. New York, Pantheon Books, 1964.

186. Ibid. Page 258.

187. Strocchia, Sharon T. "The Nun Apothecaries of Renaissance Florence: Marketing Medicines in the Convent." *Renaissance Studies* 25, no. 5 (2011): 627-47. Accessed July 14, 2021. http://www.jstor.org/stable/24420278.

188. Ibid. Page 628.

189. Ibid. Page 628.

190. Ibid. Page 631.

191. Estes, J. Worth. "The European Reception of the First Drugs from the New World." *Pharmacy in History* 37, no. 1 (1995): 3-23. Accessed July 14, 2021. http://www.jstor.org/stable/41111660.

192. Jones, Kenneth. "Review of sangre de drago (Croton lechleri)—a South American tree sap in the treatment of diarrhea, inflammation, insect bites, viral infections, and wounds: traditional uses to clinical research" https://pubmed.ncbi.nlm.nih.gov/14736360/

193. Ibid. page 632.

194. Mallon, Edward. A. M.D. "Cinchona Bark and Louis XIV." Journal of the American Medical Association JAMA. https://jamanetwork.com/journals/jama/article-abstract/327211

195. Lippi.

196. Tuke Family Collection 1660-1946. Borthwick Institute for Archives, University of York, England. https://borthcat.york.ac.uk/index.php/tuke. Accessed July 18, 2021.

197. Robertson, Emma. *Chocolate, women, and empire: A Social and Cultural History.* Manchester; Manchester University Press, 2009.

198. Chrystal, Paul; Dickinson, Joe. *History of Chocolate in York.* Pen & Sword Books. Kindle Edition.

199. Ibid. Page 20.

200. Ibid. Page 24.

201. Ibid. Page 25.

202. Strevens, Summer. "Mary Tuke: The Mother of York's Chocolate Industry" York Magazine, https://www.on-magazine.co.uk/yorkshire/history/mary-tuke-york-chocolate-industry/

203. "The Retreat, York, England." Quakers in the World. https://www.quakersintheworld.org/quakers-in-action/92/The-Retreat-York-England. Accessed July 19, 2021.

204. Waterson, Luke. "Spilling the Beans: Exploring Ecuador's Elusive Chocolate Industry." Lonely Planet, December 13, 2015. https://www.lonelyplanet.com/articles/spilling-the-beans-exploring-ecuadors-elusive-chocolate-industry. Accessed July 22, 2021.

205. Rabbi Prinz, Deborah R. *On the Chocolate Trail.* Jewish Lights Publishing, 2015.

206. Gay, James F. "Chocolate Production and Uses in 17ᵗʰ and 18ᵗʰ Century North America." *Chocolate: History, Culture, and Heritage.* Davis, California; John Wiley and Sons, Inc., 2009. Page 284.

207. Macpherson, Catherine. "Chocolate's Early History in Canada." *Chocolate: History, Culture, and Heritage.* Davis, California; John Wiley and Sons, Inc., 2009.

208. Ibid. Page 307.

209. Grivetti, Louis Evan, Shapiro, Howard-Yana. *Chocolate: History, Culture, and Heritage.* Davis, California; John Wiley and Sons, Inc., 2009.

210. Ibid. Page 54.

211. Ibid. Page 54.

212. Prinz, Page 26.

213. Ibid. Page 28.

214. Cabezon, Beatriz. Grivetti, Louis Evan. "Symbols from Ancient Times: Paleography and the St. Augustine Chocolate Saga." *Chocolate: History, and Heritage.* Davis, CA.; John Wiley and Sons, Inc. 2009.

215. Ibid. Page 691.

216. Lange, Amanda. "Baby It's Cold Outside: A Sweet History of Chocolate in New England." Historic Deerfield. https://www.historic-deerfield.org/blog/2021/1/4/baby-its-cold-outside-a-sweet-history-of-chocolate-in-new-england Accessed July 23, 2021.

217. Ward, Gerald. "Silver Chocolate Pots of Colonial Boston." *Chocolate: History, Culture and Heritage. Davis, Ca.; John Wiley and Sons, 2009.*

218. Ibid.

219.

220. Shapiro, Celia. "Nation of Nowhere." Grivetti, Louis E., Shapiro, Howard-Yana, Editors. Davis, Ca.; Wiley and Sons, 2009.

221. Ibid. Page 55.

222. Lucena, Spain. Jewish Virtual Library. https://www.jewishvirtuallibrary.org/lucena-spain-virtual-jewish-history-tour

223. Ibid.

224. Colenda Digital Repository. University of Pennsylvania. Manuscript inventory of the estate of Abraham de Lucena, a New York City Jewish merchant and minister of Shearithi Israel. Signed by William Burnet, Robert Lurting, and Rachel de Lucena. The document notes that Rachel de Lucena "being of the Hebrew Nation was duly sworn upon the Five Books of Moses." The inventory lists the deceased's property including enslaved people. Accessed July 23, 2021.

225. Gelfand, Noah L. "The Gomez Family and Atlantic Patterns in the Development of New York's Jewish Community." The Gotham Center for New York History. https://www.gothamcenter.org/blog/the-gomez-family-and-atlantic-patterns-in-the-development-of-new-yorks-jewish-community. Accessed July 25, 2021.

226. Ibid.

227. HERSHKOWITZ, LEO. "Original Inventories of Early New York Jews (1682–1763) (Concluded)." *American Jewish History* 90, no. 4 (2002): 385-448. Accessed July 24, 2021. http://www.jstor.org/stable/23887216.

228. Rabbi Prinz, Deborah. *On the Chocolate Trail.* Jewish Lights Publishing, 2015. Page 49.

229. Shapiro. Page 56.

230. Prinz, D. "A Jewish Matriarch of American Chocolate Making." May 5, 2013. https://onthechocolatetrail.org/2013/05/a-jewish-matriarch-of-american-chocolate-making/ Accessed July 25, 2021.

231. Gelfand.

232. Ibid.

233. Adverts 250 Project, https://adverts250project.org/tag/jonathan-crathorne/ Accessed July 25, 2025.

234. Adverts 250 Project, https://adverts250project.org/tag/jonathan-crathorne/ Accessed July 25, 2025.

235. Ibid.

236. Ibid.

237. Gay, James F. " Chocolate Makers in 18ᵗʰ Century Pennsylvania." *Chocolate: History, Culture, and Heritage.* Davis, Ca.; Wiley and Sons, 2009.

238 Gay. Page 393.

239. Ibid. Page 394.

240. "The Washingtons and Chocolate." https://www.mountvernon.org/inn/recipes/the-washingtons-and-chocolate/ Accessed July 25, 2021.

241. "Jefferson Quotes and Family Letters." https://tjrs.monticello.org/letter/1789 Accessed July 25, 2021.

242. *French Slave Trade.* Slavery and Remembrance, UNESCO. http://slaveryandremembrance.org/articles/article/?id=A0097 Accessed July 1, 2021.

243. Dupuy, Alex. "French Merchant Capital and Slavery in Saint-Domingue." *Latin American Perspectives* 12, no. 3 (1985): 77-102. Accessed August 1, 2021. http://www.jstor.org/stable/2633905.

244. "Lorraine Manuel Steed, digne héritiére de Modesta Testas." Le Nouvelliste. https://lenouvelliste.com/article/202730/lorraine-manuel-steed-digne-heritiere-de-modeste-testas Accessed July 31, 2021.

245. "A Report from the Rapoport Delegation on Afro-Ecuadorian Land Rights November 2009" Forgotten Territories, Unrealized Rights: Rural Afro-Ecuadorians and their Fight for Land, Equality, and Security. https://law.utexas.edu/wp-content/uploads/sites/31/2016/02/ecuador-eng.pdf Accessed July 2, 2021.

246. Cummins, Tom. "Three Gentlemen from Esmeraldas: A Portrait Fir for a King." In *Slave Portraiture in the Atlantic World.* Agnes Lugo-Ortiz, Agnes and Angela Rosenthal, eds. New York: Cambridge University Press. 2013, 119-145.

247. Ibid. Page 123.

248. "The Mulatto Gentleman of Esmeraldas." *Vistas Gallery, Accessed July 1, 2021, https:// vistasgallery.ace.fordham.edu/items/show/1903.*

249. Ibid.

250. Henderson, Paul. "Cocoa, Finance and the State in Ecuador, 1895-1925." *Bulletin of Latin American Research* 16, no. 2 (1997): 169-86. Accessed August 3, 2021. http://www. jstor.org/stable/3339105.

251. Ibid. Page 170.

252. "Ecuador's Chocolate Secret is a Sustainable Reality." Global Newswire. Jan. 6, 2010. https://www.globenewswire.com/en/news-release/2010/01/06/1254248/0/en/Ecuador-s-Chocolate-Secret-Is-a-Sustainable-Reality.html. Accessed June 30, 2021.

253. "A Report from the Rapoport Delegation on Afro-Ecuadorian Land Rights November 2009" Forgotten Territories, Unrealized Rights: Rural Afro-Ecuadorians and their Fight for Land, Equality, and Security. https://law.utexas.edu/wp-content/uploads/sites/31/2016/02/ecuador-eng.pdf Accessed July 2, 2021. Page 47.

254. Balch, Oliver. "Mars, Netlé and Hershey to face child slavery lawsuit in US." The Guardian. February 12, 2021. https://www.theguardian.com/global-development/2021/feb/12/mars-nestle-and-hershey-to-face-landmark-child-slavery-lawsuit-in-us. Accessed July 2, 2021.

255. Ibid.

256. Walt, Vivienne. "Big chocolate wins its child-labor case in Supreme Court." Fortune Magazine, June 17, 2021. https://fortune.com/2021/06/17/child-labor-case-supreme-court-big-chocolate-nestle-cargill-scotus/. Accessed July 2, 2021.

257. Ibid.

258. "Chocolate companies face new charges of child slavery." The Guardian. February 19, 2001. Freedom United. https://www.freedomunited.org/news/chocolate-companies-face-new-charges/. Accessed July 3, 2021.

259. Off, Carol. *Bitter Chocolate: Anatomy of an Industry.* New York: Random House, 2006. Page 301.

260. Robertson, Emma. *Chocolate, women, and empire: A social and cultural history.* Manchester; Manchester University Press, 2009. Page 20

261. Ibid. Page 20.

262. Ibid. Page 21.

263. "Chocolate and Feminism: Exploring the Changing Role of Women in Rowntree's Chocolate and Cocoa Advertisements, 1930-1960." *The York Historian. November 7, 2017* CHOCOLA. https://theyorkhistorian.com/2017/11/07/chocolate-and-feminism-exploring-the-changing-role-of-women-in-rowntrees-chocolate-and-cocoa-advertisements-1930-1960/. ACCESSED jULY 20, 2021.

264. Robertson. Page 21.

265. Chocolate and Feminism.

266. Robertson. Page 180.

267. Ibid.

268. MacKay, Kathryn L. "The Chocolate Dippers' Strike of 1910." Utah Historical Quarterly, Volume 83, Number 1, 2015. Utah State History. https://issuu.com/utah10/docs/uhq_volume83_2015_number1/s/10121983. Accessed July 9, 2021.

269. Ibid.

270. Ibid.

271. "Casa Amatller: The Façade of Chocolate." Patrimonio Cultural. http://patrimoni.gencat.cat/en/collection/casa-amatller

272. Instituto Amatller de Arte Hispánico. http://www.riha-institutes.org/Institutes/IAAH. Accessed July 9, 2021.

273. "How Alphonse Mucha's Iconic Posters Came to Define Art Nouveau." Artsy.net. https://www.artsy.net/article/artsy-editorial-alphonse-muchas-iconic-posters-define-art-nouveau. Accessed July 9, 2021.

274. "Advertising Posters." Mucha Foundation. http://www.muchafoundation.org/en/gallery/themes/theme/advertising-posters/object/42 Accessed July 9, 2021.

275. "Italy Enters World War I." www.theworldwar.org/learn/wwi/italy Accessed July 27, 2021.

276. Hales, Dianne. *Italy's Passionate Women: The Chocolate Maker Who Created "Baci."* https://diannehales.com/italys-passionate-women-the-chocolate-maker-who-created-baci/ Accessed July 27, 2021.

277. "The Kiss" by Francesco Hayez. Joy of Museums Virtual Tours. https://joyofmuseums.com/museums/europe/italy-museums/milan-museums/brera-art-gallery-pinacoteca-di-brera/the-kiss-by-francesco-hayez/ Accessed July 27, 2021.

278. Ibid.

279. "I Love Love Notes." Baci Perugina. https://www.baciperugina.com/intl/world/blog/news/love-notes Accessed July 27, 2021.

280. "Baci Perugina" Facts and Figures. https://www.baciperugina.com/intl/world/blog/news/facts-and-figures Accessed July 27, 2021.

281. "How Women Are Portrayed in Chocolate Advertising." Chocolate Class

282. "Naughty but Nice: Gendered Sexualization in Chocolate Advertising." Chocolate Class. https://chocolateclass.wordpress.com/2017/05/14/naughty-but-nice-gendered-sexualization-in-chocolate-advertising/. Accessed July 25, 2021.

283. Ibid.

284. Hilton, Phil. "The secrets behind advertising chocolate to women and why it's about to change forever." Stylist. https://www.stylist.co.uk/life/do-chocolate-firms-target-women-flake-cadburys-sweets-confectionery/58560. Accessed July 25, 2021.

285. "The Benefits of Having a Healthy Relationship with Chocolate." Johns Hopkins Medicine. https://www.hopkinsmedicine.org/health/wellness-and-prevention/the-benefits-of-having-a-healthy-relationship-with-chocolate. Accessed July 25, 2021.

286. Gunnars, Kris. "7 Proven Health Benefits of Dark Chocolate." Healthline. https://www.healthline.com/nutrition/7-health-benefits-dark-chocolate#TOC_TITLE_HDR_5

287. Ibid.

288. D'Souza, Romana. "Why Women Should East Chocolate." India Times. https://www.indiatimes.com/health/healthyliving/why-women-should-eat-more-chocolate-242166.html. Accessed July 28, 2021.

289. "Cocoa bean DNA testing offers path to end slavery and child labour in chocolate industry."

290. Ibid.

291. "Which Countries Eat the Most Chocolate." World Atlas. https://www.worldatlas.com/articles/which-countries-eat-the-most-chocolate.html Accessed August 1, 2021.

292. "Crazy Valentine Day's Facts." Gourmet Gift Baskets. https://www.gourmetgiftbaskets.com/Blog/post/crazy-valentines-day-facts.aspx Accessed July 21, 2021.

Acknowledgments

THIS BOOK ON THE CULTURAL HISTORY OF CHOCOLATE HAS BEEN DECADES IN the making. From my childhood spent in Ecuador, chocolate's country of origin, to my 65 years of extensive international travel to the most delectable chocolate centers worldwide, I've had a love affair with chocolate. Many of the people who've shared with me their love—and deep knowledge of chocolate— are now deceased, but the memories of our joyful times together remain as sweet as ever.

I'm indebted to the scholars who continue to study every aspect of chocolate, and share their respective academic findings in this field. It is their knowledge that has added gravitas to this book. However, the heart and soul of this volume are the indigenous women who cultivated cacao in the Amazonian rain forest of my ancestral land, and through their original and steadfast dedication to cacao, these women continued to forge a link with the people of Mesoamerica, and subsequently with the world.

I am most grateful for the encouragement and enthusiasm for my writing life that I constantly receive from my family and friends. The list is long and deep, but foremost is my immediate family. Thank you for your love and support.

Connie Spenuzza M.S. Ed., received First Place from the International Latino Book Awards for her novels *Lucia Zárate* (2017), *Missing in Machu Picchu* (2013) and *Traces of Bliss* (2012). Her travel memoir *Jubilant Journeys* (2019) was awarded Second Place, following first place winner and Nobel Peace Prize nominee José Andrés. The Association of American Publishers and the Las Comadres International organization selected her novels to the National Latino Book Club. In 2017, Foreword Reviews selected *Lucía Zárate* as Indie Book Finalist, *Parisian Promises* (2014) was the runner-up for the Paris Book Award and *Gathering the Indigo Maidens* (2011) was a finalist for the Mariposa Award. Her children's bilingual fables: *Olinguito Speaks Up* was endorsed by the Smithsonian Institution, *Lalo Loves to Help,* and *Howl of the Mission Owl* have received numerous awards. Her pen name for the works above is Cecilia Velástegui. Her 2021 art history book: *Spanish Colonial Paintings Paired with European Engravings,* debuted with an immersive multimedia exhibit at the California landmark Mission San Juan Capistrano.

Connie was born in Ecuador and raised in California and France. She received her graduate degree from the University of Southern California, speaks four languages, and has traveled to 127 countries. Connie donates the proceeds from the sale of her books to the fight against human trafficking. She lives in Dana Point, California.

www.ConnieSpenuzza.com

Turpin. P.

Lambert J.e sculp.

CACAO.

a. l. l.